The Revolt
of the Widows

The Social World of the Apocryphal Acts

BY STEVAN L. DAVIES

SOUTHERN ILLINOIS UNIVERSITY PRESS
CARBONDALE AND EDWARDSVILLE

FEFFER & SIMONS, INC.
LONDON AND AMSTERDAM

Printed in the United States of America.

Designed by Bob Nance

Library of Congress Cataloging in Publication Data

Davies, Stevan L   1948–
  The revolt of the widows.

  Bibliography: p.
  Includes index.
  1. Bible. N.T. Apocryphal books. Acts—
Criticism, interpretation, etc.   I. Title.
BS2871.D38   229′.92095   80-11331
ISBN 0-8093-0958-0

To my wife, Sally, my parents, and my sister

Contents

Acknowledgments

PERMISSION of the publishers to quote from the titles listed below is gratefully acknowledged:

E. J. Brill for permission to quote from A. F. J. Klijn, *The Acts of Thomas*, 1962; Peter M. Peterson, *Andrew, Brother of Simon Peter*, 1958; and Gilles Quispel, *Makarius, das Thomasevangelium und das Lied von der Perle*, 1967.

University of California Press and Faber and Faber, Ltd., for permission to quote from Peter Brown, *Religion and Society in the Age of St. Augustine*, 1972.

Cambridge University Press for permission to quote from E. R. Dodds, *Pagan and Christian in an Age of Anxiety*, 1965.

The University of Chicago Press for permission to quote from Adolph Jensen, *Myth and Cult among Primitive Peoples*, 1963.

Wm. B. Eerdmans Publishing Company for permission to quote from W. A. Craigie, trans., "The Acts of Xanthippe and Polyxena," in *The Ante-Nicene Library, Additional Volume*, edited by Allan Menzies, 1896, and M. B. Riddle, "Two Epistles Concerning Virginity." Vol. 8 in *The Ante-Nicene Christian Fathers*, edited by A. Roberts and J. Donaldson, 1951.

Harper & Row, Publishers, Inc., and E. J. Brill for permission to quote from James M. Robinson, ed., *The Nag Hammadi Library*, 1977.

The Liturgical Press for permission to quote from Roger Gryson, *The Ministry of Women in the Early Church*, 1976. Copyrighted by The Order of St. Benedict, Inc., Collegeville, Minnesota.

Lutterworth Press and The Westminster Press for permission to quote from *New Testament Apocrypha*, 2 vols., edited by Wilhelm Schneemelcher and Edgar Hennecke. English translation by R. McL. Wilson. Published in Great Britain by Lutterworth Press, 1965. Published in the United States by The Westminster Press, 1966. Copyright © 1964 by J. C. B. Mohr (Paul Siebeck), Tübingen.

David McKay Company, Inc., for permission to quote from J. N. D. Kelly, *Early Christian Creeds*, 1960

Macmillan Publishing Co., Inc., for permission to quote from Mary Lawrence McKenna, *Women of the Church*, 1967.

Manchester University Press for permission to quote from Maxwell Marwick, *Sorcery in Its Social Setting*, 1965.

McGraw-Hill Book Company for permission to quote from Lucy Mair, *Witchcraft*, 1969.

Moody Press for permission to quote from Charles Ryrie, *The Role of Women in the Church*, 1958.

Oxford University Press for permission to quote from Max Weber, *From Max Weber, Essays in Sociology*, edited and translated by H. H. Garth and C. W. Mills, 1958.

Princeton University Press for permission to quote from Max Pulver, "Jesus' Round Dance and Crucifixion According to the Acts of John." Vol. 2 in *The Mysteries: Papers from the Eranos Yearbooks*, edited by Joseph Campbell. Bollingen Series. 30 vols. 1955.

Random House, Inc., for permission to quote from Elaine Pagels, *The Gnostic Gospels*, 1979.

Routledge & Kegan Paul, Ltd., for permission to quote from Mary Douglas, *Purity and Danger*, 1966.

Scholar's Press for permission to quote from Pheme Perkins, "Peter in Gnostic Revelation." Vol. 2 in *Society of Biblical Literature 1974 Seminar Papers*, edited by George MacRae, 1974.

Simon & Schuster for permission to quote from Rosemary Radford Ruether, ed., "Virginal Feminism in the Fathers of the Church," in *Religion and Sexism*, 1974, and *Women of Spirit*, 1979.

University of Notre Dame Press for permission to quote from Paul J. Achtemeier, "Jesus and the Disciples As Miracle Workers in the Apocryphal New Testament." In *Aspects of Religious Propaganda in Judaism and Early Christianity*, edited by Elisabeth Schüssler Fiorenza, 1976.

The Revolt of the Widows

I

Introduction

DURING the end of the second and the beginning of the third centuries in the eastern part of the Roman Empire, some Christians wrote, for other Christians, lengthy stories featuring the apostles. Substantial portions of those stories, similar in many respects to ancient Hellenistic romances, have survived to this day and are known as the apocryphal Acts of the Apostles.

The apocryphal Acts are evidence for a form of Christian life at an early stage of Christian history. Although the authors of the Acts drew upon existing legendary material from both Christian and non-Christian tradition, their creativity is not thereby negated. They had to select some material and reject the rest, shape the legends into Christian tales, write new material of their own, and combine all these elements into a single coherent work. Our concern is with how these borrowed and created materials are used in the Acts. No author writes in a vacuum, all transform what they know to produce something new. We shall examine the Acts as they stand to discover what they reveal about the social circumstances of their composition and their compilers.

There is an important distinction between diachronic and synchronic inquiry. Diachronic inquiry, like etymology, traces forms back in time. Synchronic inquiry, like the reading of a sentence, is the endeavor to comprehend the meaning of forms as they are found together at a particular time. This investigation is synchronic and its time is the period at the end of the second and the beginning of the third centuries.

Most of the sources used in this study appear in English translation in Montague R. James's *The Apocryphal New Testament* and in volume two of Edgar Hennecke and Wilhelm Schneemelcher's *New Testament Apocrypha*.[1] Hennecke and Schneemelcher's book is more than a collection of readable translations. It contains essays by competent authorities on each of the apocryphal Acts and, what is more important, considerable technical discussion of the processes through which texts for translation were critically selected. To the extent presently possible the materials in the second volume of *New Testament Apocrypha* are reliable and come from the late second and early third centuries.

The Acts of Xanthippe is only available in W. A. Craigie's translation found in the additional volume of the *Ante-Nicene Christian Writers* series.[2] The references and quotations of material in the apocryphal Acts refer to Hennecke and Schneemelcher's work and to Craigie's translation of the Acts of Xanthippe. For convenience we shall use the following abbreviations for references and quotations of apocryphal Acts:

The Acts of John, A.Jn.
The Acts of Peter, A.Pt.
The Acts of Paul, A.Pl.
The Acts of Andrew, A.An.
The Acts of Thomas, A.Th.
The Acts of Xanthippe, A.Xn.

For the most part the Acts are divided into numbered chapters in Hennecke and Schneemelcher's work, and we will follow their practice in our citations, for example (A.Jn. 43). Following Hennecke and Schneemelcher's usage, we abbreviate sources of the

1. James, *Apocryphal New Testament*, pp. 228–438; Schneemelcher and Hennecke, eds., *New Testament Apocrypha*, vol. 2, English trans., ed. R. McL. Wilson, pp. 167–531.
2. Craigie, *The Ante-Nicene Christian Library, Additional Volume*, ed. Allan Menzies, pp. 204–17.

fragmentary material which survives from the original Acts of Andrew as follows:

Codex Vaticanus gracae 808, A.An. Cod. Vat.
Papyrus Coptic Utrecht 1, A.An. Utrecht
Narratio, A.An. Narr.
Martyrium I, II, etc., A.An. Mart.
Laudatio, A.An. Laud.

Similarly, material from the *Martyrium* of the Acts of Thomas is abbreviated A.Th. Mart.

For the Acts of Xanthippe we will refer to the divisions in Craigie's translation, e.g. (A.Xn. 12). We shall cite material available in Montague R. James's translations as follows: (A.An. 6, James). Because Gregory of Tours's précis of the Acts of Andrew is greatly censored and altered toward orthodoxy, we shall draw very little evidence from that source.[3] When they can tell us about the general practice and world view of Christians of early centuries, we will use evidence from the writings of the Church Fathers to supplement that in the Acts. To avoid confusion, whenever we have occasion to refer to the canonical Acts of the Apostles we shall use that full title.

Our study begins where that of Rosa Söder, author of an outstanding book on the literary form of the apocryphal Acts, left off. On the final page of her book she wrote:

The apocryphal Acts are popular stories intended for the common people and not so much for the educated, as was the novel. This, however, does not exclude the possibility that the authors, for their own purposes of providing instruction through entertainment, also made use, occasionally excessive use, of the means available during their times. This, again, would be a sign of the popular character of the author himself.[4]

We are concerned with the people who form the community behind the Acts because, in the words of Wilhelm Schneemelcher, "the apocryphal Acts are the most important witnesses to the re-

3. James, *Apocryphal New Testament*, pp. 337–49.
4. Söder, *Die apokryphen Apostelgeschichten und die romanhafte Literatur der Antique*, p. 216; see also R. Reitzenstein, *Hellenistiche Wundererzählungen*.

ligious ideals of a great part of the Christian race, ideals which did not always follow the paths which were later considered acceptable to the Christian Church. An acquaintance with these religious ideals, however, is beyond question of the utmost importance for the historical understanding of conditions in the Church of the Second and Third Centuries."[5]

The apocryphal Acts with which we are particularly concerned are those generally considered to be of earliest date: the Acts of John, Peter, Paul, Andrew, and Thomas. We intend to add to this list the Acts of Xanthippe, which has been considered to be of somewhat later date than the others, according to an argument made by Montague R. James.[6] We will endeavor to show that his argument is too weak to be of value.

There is a substantial consensus on the dates of five apocryphal Acts. James dates the Acts of John at "not later than the middle of the second century," the Acts of Paul from circa 160–170, the Acts of Peter at "about the year 200," the Acts of Andrew "well after 200; even after 250 perhaps," and the Acts of Thomas from "the third century."[7]

A. F. J. Klijn, in his book entitled *The Acts of Thomas*, writes that "if the Acts of Paul go back to a time round about the year 190, the Acts of Peter were written about the year 175. It is possible that the Acts of John are of about the same date."[8] He also finds that "the Acts of Thomas show the closest relation with the Acts of Peter. If this means that the Acts of Thomas are dependent on the Acts of Peter, the Acts of Thomas were written in the beginning of the third century."[9]

Klijn's conclusion is in accord with that of Gilles Quispel who, in

---

5. Schneemelcher and Hennecke, eds., *New Testament Apocrypha*, pp. 117–18; cf. James, *Apocryphal New Testament*, who says of the Acts: "If they are not good sources of history in one sense, they are in another. They record the imaginations, hopes, and fears of the men who wrote them; they show what was acceptable to the unlearned Christians of the first ages, what interested them, what they admired, what ideals of conduct they cherished for this life, what they thought they would find in the next" (p. xiii).

6. James, "Acta Xanthippae et Polyxenae," *Apocrypha Anecdota, Texts and Studies*, vol. 3, no. 2, pp. 43–85.

7. James, *Apocryphal New Testament*, p. 228.

8. Klijn, *The Acts of Thomas*, p. 23.

9. Ibid., p. 26.

Makarius, das Thomasevangelium und das Lied von der Perle, writes that the Acts of Thomas "were written in Edessa sometime around the year 225 A.D." [10] The Acts of Peter was, in the opinion of Léon Vouaux, "composed in Asia in the first years of the third century. Any determination more precise than this will be arbitrary." [11] Writing more generally, R. A. Lipsius concludes that "the gnostic Acts of Peter and Paul were already demonstrably being read in the second century, while those of John were probably being read at that time." [12] The Acts of Thomas he dates "probably before the middle of the third century." [13]

In *Andrew, Brother of Simon Peter*, Peter M. Peterson, the most recent authority quoted here, writes that "the Acts of Paul, then, were composed in the decade 190–200 at the very latest. However, the Acts of Paul are later than the Acts of Peter which must therefore be from the previous decade (or earlier) viz. 180–190." He continues, "If the dating of Peter (at the latest) is to be accepted as 180–190, then, it follows that the Acts of Andrew (whose definitely Gnostic origin speaks for an early date) were somewhat later, perhaps 190–200." Peterson agrees that the Acts of John comes from circa 150. [14] Quispel, also writing on the Acts of Andrew, regards it as an open question whether that document was not of earlier date than the Acts of Peter. [15]

Various essays in Hennecke and Schneemelcher's second volume on the New Testament apocrypha suggest proposed dates. K. Schäferdiek believes that a date as late as the third century cannot be completely ruled out for the Acts of John. [16] Schneemelcher writes that the Acts of Peter "must have originated before ca. 190, perhaps in the decade 180–190," and that for the Acts of Paul "the period between 185–195 may be regarded as a possible estimate." [17] G. Bornkamm believes Thomas is from the first half of the third cen-

---

10. Quispel, *Makarius, das Thomasevangelium und das Lied von der Perle*, p. 39.

11. Vouaux, *Les Actes de Pierre*, p. 108.

12. Lipsius, *Die apokryphen Apostelgeschichten und Apostellegenden*, vol. 1, p. 4.

13. Ibid., p. 5.

14. Peterson, *Andrew, Brother of Simon Peter: His History and His Legends*, pp. 25–26.

15. Quispel, "An Unknown Fragment of the Acts of Andrew," *Vigiliae Christianae* 10(1956):147.

16. Schneemelcher and Hennecke, eds., *New Testament Apocrypha*, pp. 214–15.

17. Ibid., p. 275.

tury and M. Hornschuh places the Acts of Andrew "in the second half of the [second] century but not after 190." [18]

The consensus of scholarship is clear. The five best-known Acts were probably composed during the latter part of the second century and the first half of the third century, circa A.D. 160–225.

To the list of Acts composed in Greek in the region of Asia Minor and Greece between the years 160–225 should be added the Acts of Xanthippe, which also is known as the Acts of Xanthippe and Polyxena. This document has been erroneously placed later in time because of M. R. James's assertion that it is dependent on the Acts of Philip. James's argument is but one paragraph long. He makes five points:

1. That "the introduction of Philip as an actor in our book is a principal reason for supposing that the Acts of Philip were known to the author."

2. That Philip is found to be in Greece both in the Acts of Xanthippe and in a portion of Philip's Acts.

3. That there is allusion to Philip's tunic in both documents.

4. That in the Acts of Philip a great light shines around Philip's head and in the Acts of Xanthippe Paul has a shining inscription on his forehead.

5. That there is a talking leopard in the Acts of Philip and a talking lioness in the Acts of Xanthippe. [19]

Of his first point we need only say that the existence of an Apostle named Philip would be known to a reader of the canonical Acts of the Apostles. Use of a particular name, one that was known throughout the Christian movement, does not indicate knowledge of a document featuring a person of that name unless evidence is clearly present for the use of that document.

It is just as reasonable to postulate that the fact that the Acts of Philip locates Philip in Greece stemmed from a general notion to that effect in Christian tradition, as to suppose that the general notion was brought about through the existence of a particular document.

Philip's tunic is a matter of discussion in the Acts of Philip for it was decreed that he should wear such garb by Jesus himself. In the

18. Ibid., pp. 441, 397.
19. James, "Acta Xanthippae," p. 52.

Acts of Xanthippe (A.Xn. 25) Philip's tunic is mentioned but once, in passing, and it is in the possession of another man. The garment itself receives no particular attention.

The notion that Paul has a shining inscription on his forehead in the Acts of Xanthippe (A.Xn. 8) could be traced to the Acts of Paul (A.Pl. 3:3) wherein Paul is said to have the face of an angel or, indeed, to the Acts of the Apostles (6:15) where the same notion is present. There is no apparent relationship of dependence between Philip's shining countenance and letters appearing on Paul's brow. One might just as easily argue that such a notion comes from the shining inscription reported to have appeared miraculously in the book of Daniel (5:24–26).

Finally, there is a talking lion in the Acts of Paul (A.Pl. 7), a document that the author of the Acts of Xanthippe did demonstrably use. The talking leopard in Philip's Acts may well be another reflection of the same verbal feline found in the Acts of Paul.

There is no doubt that the author of the Acts of Xanthippe draws clearly and directly from the Acts of Paul and the Acts of Peter; James's evidence on that score is conclusive. In general an author who borrows from other documents will either attempt to disguise sources or will leave them readily apparent. The dependence of the Acts of Xanthippe on the Acts of Paul and the Acts of Peter is clearly apparent. Use of the Acts of Andrew, Thomas, and Philip is never clear; in fact we see no reason to assume anything more than that apostles named Andrew and Philip were known to the author of the Acts of Xanthippe, and that those who comprised the community behind the apocryphal Acts shared several general notions and styles of speaking, some of which appear in more than one document.

A. F. J. Klijn, having considered the question of whether or not the Acts of Thomas is dependent on other Acts, says: "The conclusion of this survey is that sometimes the same ideas are met in Apocryphal Acts. Whether these ideas go back to a mutual dependency or to a common background is difficult to say. In most cases we are dealing with a common background available also in the canonical Acts, in other cases with standard phrases and examples taken from the preaching of the church."[20] James's assertion that

---

20. Klijn, *The Acts of Thomas*, p. 26.

the Acts of Xanthippe depends on Philip, Andrew, and Thomas does no more than point to certain similarities in style and tone and to an occasional motif which is possibly (never definitely) present in both Xanthippe and one of the other three. He proves nicely that the Acts of Xanthippe comes from the same milieu of ideas as the other Acts; its literary dependence and later date remain entirely unproven. The Acts of Xanthippe probably originated in the same region and at the same period as did the Acts of Andrew and the Acts of Thomas, that is, circa A.D. 190–225 in the eastern part of the Roman Empire.

The Acts that were composed in Greek (Paul, Peter, John, Andrew, and Xanthippe) probably stem from Greece and Asia Minor. There is no reason to dispute Tertullian's statement that the Acts of Paul was composed in Asia Minor.[21] The Acts of Peter, in James's opinion, was probably written "by a resident in Asia Minor (he does not know much about Rome) not later than A.D. 200 in Greek."[22] Peterson agrees with Flamion that the Acts of Andrew was possibly composed in Achaia, "certainly in Greece or Asia Minor. That the Acts of Peter and those of John, attributed to Anatolian authorship, were the predecessors of the Acts of Andrew would indicate origin from this general region."[23] The Acts of John was probably written by a resident of Asia Minor; R. A. Lipsius calls this document, specifically, the "Ephesian Acts of John," while Schäferdiek says that it is possibly from that region.[24] As the predecessors of the Acts of Xanthippe, the Acts of Peter and of Paul, are from Anatolia or Greece we may safely assume that the Acts of Xanthippe also stems from that area.

Although James is not at all convinced that the Acts of Thomas was originally written in Syriac, most modern scholars are. It therefore seems most likely that the Acts of Thomas originated in Roman Syria.[25]

21. Tertullian *De Baptismo*, p. 17.

22. James, *Apocryphal New Testament*, p. 300.

23. Peterson, *Andrew*, p. 29.

24. Lipsius, *Die apokryphen Apostelgeschichten*, p. 10; Schneemelcher and Hennecke, eds., *New Testament Apocrypha*, p. 214.

25. See, for example, Klijn, *Acts of Thomas*, p. 13; but see also James, *Apocryphal New Testament*, who writes: "It is, I believe, still arguable (though denied by the Syriacists) that here is a relic of the original Greek text: in other words, the Acts *were*

All of the Acts, except Thomas's, seem to come from Asia Minor or Greece. It is not necessary for our purposes to achieve more specificity than this; indeed, much more specificity is probably impossible.

Scholars often dismiss the Acts from serious consideration as evidence about Christians of the first centuries of the church. In doing so they dismiss a substantial percentage of all early Christian documents. A moment's reflection will reveal that we have little more than the canonical writings, the Apologists, Irenaeus, Clement, Tertullian, and a handful of letters remaining from the first two centuries, if we exclude the apocryphal material. But if we include it, would we be including nothing but ridiculous pseudo-history originating from the disturbed minds of unhappy heretics? No, we would be including the testimony of Christians, of people who were neither heresiarchs nor sophisticated theologians. The apocryphal Acts are testimonies to varieties of Christian belief and to a particular way of life. They derive from common people who agreed on the proper way of living for Christians but had differing doctrinal opinions.

Variation in doctrine, however, was as characteristic of Christians of the second century as it is of Christians in America today. Walter Bauer has shown that early Christianity was a continuum of ideas rather than the struggle of a band of true orthodox believers against a world of heretics.[26] Each of the apocryphal Acts has its place in that continuum of ideas; M. R. James has taken the trouble to pronounce on the orthodoxy of several Acts and finds that Paul is orthodox, while Peter is less so but more than John.[27]

Such judgments really tell us very little. We must not expect the Acts to resemble the productions of theologically learned individuals; rather, they are the expressions of the beliefs and life-styles of some of the "simple" people. M. Hornschuh, discussing the Acts of Andrew, says in agreement with G. Quispel that "an author, belonging to the church in the second century could have gone as far

composed in Greek, and early rendered into Syriac. Becoming scarce or being wholly lost in Greek they were retranslated out of Syriac into Greek. But meanwhile the original Greek of the Martyrdom had survived separately, and we have it here. This was M. Bonnet's view and it is one which I should like to adopt" (p. 364).

26. Bauer, *Rechtglaubigkeit und Ketzerei im ältesten Christentum*.
27. James, *Apocryphal New Testament*, pp. 270, 300.

in the acceptance of foreign thought as the author of [the Acts of Andrew] has done without thereby stepping beyond the bounds of what was still possible within the catholic church."[28] About the Acts of Paul, Schneemelcher writes that "the author makes the apostle the herald of a very simple faith, which can be reduced to a few formulae and presents very clear positions against Gnostic speculation, rejection of the Old Testament, denial of the resurrection and relaxation of ethical standards."[29] The compositors of Andrew's and Paul's Acts were members of the primitive Christian church, and their various opinions are indicative not of warring schools but of a permissible diversity of belief.

Concerning the Acts of Peter, Schneemelcher writes: "It may probably be said that the circles in which the Acts of Peter originated were especially interested in [sexual chastity]. It is well known that encratite ethics and docetic christology often go together. But the combination of docetic pronouncements and encratite trends is not enough to prove the gnostic character of the Acts of Peter. It is rather the popular piety of the second and third century that here presents itself. Here, as in every age, disparate elements are brought together which the theologians tend to keep carefully apart."[30] It would be a fatal error, then, to impose our customary theological categories upon the apocryphal Acts. "It is a mark of this popular literature, and one which heightens its importance to the historian, that it can combine in itself both Catholic and Gnostic elements."[31] If one text is, from our viewpoint, more gnostic or more orthodox than another, this means only that different persons writing for the Christian church had somewhat different opinions.

On one matter all apocryphal Acts are agreed: that sexual intercourse should not be a part of Christian life. Schneemelcher puts it this way: "One of the most distinctive features of these works is that they are not determined by theological reflections but rather directed by practical intentions. Thus the encratite strain that occurs in different forms in the several apocryphal Acts should undoubtedly be understood as showing that the authors of these Acts

28. Schneemelcher and Hennecke, eds., *New Testament Apocrypha*, p. 392.
29. Ibid., p. 350.
30. Ibid., p. 275.
31. Ibid., p. 177.

took sexual continence to be an essential feature, or sometimes indeed the authentic content, of the Christian message."[32] This absolute rejection of sexual intercourse is often said to be characteristic of "Encratites," a term we shall refrain from using in this study. It is not wholly inaccurate if defined as in the *Encyclopedia of Religion and Ethics*: "Christians of the early Church who made abstinence from flesh, wine, marriage and possessions their rule of life. . . . Without holding one form of creed or being organized as a body, they practiced everywhere the same kind of asceticism. Their spirit was widely diffused."[33] However, the ingrained tendency of scholarship everywhere is to assume that a specific term describes a specific sect. The "Encratites" behind the Acts are not a sect of Christians but Christians of a particular life-style existing in a church made up of ascetic and nonascetic people. Further, Encratism is often taken to imply a form of gnosticism. If it is true that "most Encratites were philosophical dualists" and "denied the identity of the supreme God with the Creator of the world," then the apocryphal Acts are not Encratite at all.[34] The Acts of Paul, in fact, attacks that view directly (A.Pl. 8:3).

Our quarrel is not with the term "Encratite" as applied to the Acts by careful scholars who use it to describe a form of life and not a set of beliefs. Rather, we find the term too suggestive of inaccuracy to be worthy of use when better terminology is available. We will describe the Acts simply as the products of communities of sexually continent Christians, a lengthier description but less likely to mislead.

In their stress on asceticism and continence the apocryphal Acts are by no means unique in the ancient world. There survive a number of fictionalized lives of men portrayed as heroes of virtue and self-denial (e.g., Philostratus's Life of Apollonius of Tyana and Lucian's writing about Demonax the Cynic) and lives of traveling ascetics written from an attitude of disapproval (e.g., Lucian's exposé of the "Christian" Peregrinus Proteus and his Life of Alexander of Abonoteichus). Further, the moralistic Sentences of Sextus and Sentences of Pythagoras resemble the Acts in their stress on self-denial for religious ends. Although such works are interesting in

32. Ibid., p. 172.
33. *Encyclopedia of Religion and Ethics*, s.v. "Encratites."
34. Ibid.

themselves and certainly relevant to the attempt to understand the social climate of ancient times, they will not be considered in detail in the present book. They show a more moderate and less alienated face to the world than do the apocryphal Acts. In E. R. Dodds's words:

The major difference between pagan and Christian asceticism can best be appreciated by looking at the Sentences of Sextus, a collection of religious and moral aphorisms which survives both in the form given to it by a Christian redactor about the end of the second century and also in several older pagan versions. The asceticism of the pagan aphorisms is moderate, not to say banal: self-control is the foundation of piety; we should eat only when hungry, sleep only when we must, avoid getting drunk, and have sex relations only for child-getting. But on the last point the Christian redactor takes a much grimmer view: marriage, if ventured on at all, should be a "competition in continence", and self-castration is preferable to impurity. Such opinions were widely held, and sometimes acted on, by Christian and Gnostic rigorists. Both Galen and Origen testify that many contemporary Christians abstained from sex relations throughout their lives; virginity was "the supreme and crowning achievement"; the widely read Acts of Paul and Thecla taught that only virgins will be resurrected. . . .[35]

The asceticism Philostratus attributes to his hero (Apollonius) is by contemporary Christian standards quite moderate.[36]

In some respects such works as Philostratus's Life of Apollonius and what are called the Acts of Pagan Martyrs seem to glorify men who were as opposed to civil authority as were the authors of the Acts. In fact these non-Christian writings speak out in opposition to a particular "tyrannical" form of Roman government opposed by some of the educated Roman elite. They show much less general social alienation than do the apocryphal Acts. Ramsay MacMullen, in his *Enemies of the Roman Order*, has done an outstanding study of these and related pagan writings. In their asceticism the Acts are not unique, but are extreme even for their time. The purpose of this study is not to survey the history of early Christian asceticism but

35. Dodds, *Pagan and Christian in an Age of Anxiety*, p. 32.
36. Ibid., p. 34, n.2.

to learn as much as we can about the social world of the apocryphal Acts from the Acts themselves. For the history of early Christian asceticism the reader may refer to the standard works.[37]

In this study we are exploring a type of literature; if we can clarify some of the questions and factors common to the Acts, it will be valuable then to proceed to investigate each of them separately. Each of the Acts is unquestionably distinct from the others in some aspects and in details of theology, narrative structure, and world view. But each is also aligned with the others in general and it is on this level of generality that our study is made. It is our intention to study the early apocryphal Acts as a collection and thereby lay a foundation for later studies of each of the Acts separately.

To investigate the social world of the apocryphal Acts we must make the fundamental assumption, or adopt the methodological principle, that in writing pious fiction people model the imaginative world about which they write on the real social world in which they live.[38] It seems probable that the problems and difficulties described in the Acts, particularly those not successfully resolved, reflect problems and difficulties experienced, but not yet resolved, by the community from which the Acts derive.

At first glance the apocryphal Acts are difficult documents to take seriously. They are imaginative, at times even grotesque, compendiums of miracles, conversions, and adventures. Fundamentally hyperbolic, they are filled with obvious exaggerations, extravagant statements and fabulous journeys. For example, the Acts assume that in the time of the Apostles all opposition could be overcome and entire cities converted to the faith overnight. The Acts derive, however, from a social world—a structure of human relationships and values on which their world of fantasy is erected. A social world is a network of relationships between leaders and followers, men and women, rulers and rebels, wives and husbands,

---

37. See, among others, H. Chadwick, "Enkrateia" in the *Reallexicon für Antike und Christentum*, vol. 5; H. von Campenhausen, *Die Askese im Urchristentum*; A. Vööbius, *A History of Asceticism in the Syrian Orient*.

38. See the Archbishop of Canterbury's Committee on the Ministry of Women, which expressed the opinion that, while the Acts may not be of direct historical value, they are of value, "as affording evidence of the condition of the community in which they were produced, and for whose edification they were intended" (*The Ministry of Women*, Appendix 4, p. 78); also see notes 5 and 27 above.

etc. By focusing on such relationships, we may see through the Acts' hyperbole and fantasy and uncover the framework of reality on which the tales in the Acts are constructed. Since the Acts are so intrinsically hyperbolic we will not make a case for any particular kind of relationship unless at least two different Acts provide instances of it. We will focus not on a few crucial details but on themes which are repeated.

In referring to the "community" behind the apocryphal Acts, we do not wish to postulate or seem to postulate anything like a structured social organization or institutional system opposed to an "orthodox" church. Rather, "community" is used here simply to indicate persons with a similar outlook on life and religion. Because there is considerable stylistic and conceptual similarity among the apocryphal Acts, we judge that they were shared within a dispersed circle of persons who appreciated them and whose interests and concerns they reflect.

In seeking to determine what kind of Christian person predominated in the community behind the Acts, we will assume that the kind of person for whom the Acts were intended was the focus of the Acts' primary concern and of their edifying intention. The apocryphal Acts, it will be shown, were not written primarily for Christians in general but for Christians of a particular kind.

There will be three parts to this study. In chapters 2 and 3 we will investigate the magical world view of late second-century Christendom and look into the relationships between itinerant wonder-working Christian preachers (who were, as we shall show, sometimes known as "apostles" in the second century) and their audiences, the people they converted and to whom they preached. This discussion will set the stage for the more specific inquiries of later chapters. In chapters 4 and 5 our focus will be on the persons the Acts describe as new Christian converts, with the assumption that the characteristics of these central non-"apostolic" figures in the Acts can, when carefully considered, allow us to determine the probable original community from which the Acts derived. We will continue that line of argument in our sixth chapter, in an effort to determine who might most probably have written the apocryphal Acts. If we can never claim to reach firm and indubitable conclusions, we can at least arrive at the most probable hypotheses.

II

The Magical World View of Antiquity

BEFORE we turn to consideration of apostles in the apocryphal Acts, we will examine the magical world view of antiquity. If we are to take the Acts seriously we must realize that magic and miracle, dismissed today as superstition, were taken to be a part of reality in the period circa A.D. 160–225. The Acts exaggerate magical healings, resuscitations from the dead, miracles performed by remarkable men. These accounts are only exaggerations, however, and not (in terms of the second century) sheer fantasies. At that time healings, resuscitations, and miracles were considered to be possible.

The word "magic" presents a terminological problem. Among historians and anthropologists "magic" can be a technical term referring to the supposed manipulation of reality by spells, special words of power, and incantations, with no ethical or pejorative connotation. For the most part we shall use "magic" in this sense. A second use of the term "magic," as an accusation to launch against an opponent, will be examined later in this chapter. "Sorcery" will *always* be used in its sense of accusation, while "charismatic action" will occasionally be used to mean the manipulation of supernatural power by humans when the word "magic" might seem to imply something pejorative.

In the ancient world magic was accepted as a fact of everyday

17

life. The environment was thought to be filled with spiritual beings, both beneficent and maleficent, in the same way that it was
filled with dogs, flies, and sparrows (and in much the same way as
we think our environment is filled with bacteria and viruses). For
Tertullian the centers of social life, the circuses and temples and fo-
rums, are seemingly as well populated with demons as they are
with people, demons which can be "everywhere in a single moment. The whole world is as one place to them."[1] He writes that
"the amphitheater is consecrated to names more numerous and
more dire than is the capitol itself, temple of all demons as it is.
There are as many unclean spirits there as it holds men."[2] Further,
"even the streets and the market-place and the baths and the taverns
and our very dwelling places are not free altogether from idols.
Satan and his angels have filled the whole world."[3]

In a world filled with such creatures men sought to control and
use them. E. R. Dodds, in *Pagan and Christian in an Age of Anxiety*,
states that "virtually every one, pagan, Jewish, Christian or Gnostic, believed in the existence of these beings and in their function as
mediators, whether he called them daemons or angels or aions or
simply 'spirits'. In the eyes of many pious pagans even the gods of
Greek mythology were by this time no more than mediating daemons, satraps of an invisible supramundane King. And the
'daemonic man', who knew how to establish contact with them,
was correspondingly esteemed."[4] An apostle or wonder-worker
who claimed to be capable of using spiritual powers and had some
evidence to back him up was a force to be reckoned with.

Magic became a sort of technology, a science of demon-hus-
bandry. The magic papyri are forceful evidence that magical spells
and procedures were common and widespread.[5] Further evidence
is provided by the amulets, lead curse tablets, and ostraca inscribed
with magical formulas that have been recovered from the ancient
world.

1. Tertullian *Apologeticus* 22.
2. Tertullian *De Spectaculis* 12.
3. Tertullian *De Spectaculis* 8.
4. Dodds, *Pagan and Christian in an Age of Anxiety*, p. 38.
5. See, for example, Karl Preisendanz, *Papyri Graecae Magicae*, vols. 1–2; Erwin
Goodenough, *Jewish Symbols in the Greco-Roman Period*, vol. 4; and Angelicus M.
Kropp, *Ausgewählte Koptische Zaubertexte*, vols. 1–2.

Magic was not only discussed in religious circles, it was a recognized category of criminal activity in law. However, even the
ruling classes indulged in magic. Ramsay MacMullen notes this peculiar dichotomy between the common practice and official disapproval of magic. "Set against the whole picture of magic in Roman
society the official attitude is a plain contradiction—resolved, however, by the very importance of magic. Not only could it not be
eradicated from the common mind but the most enlightened people
took it seriously, attributing to it (they would have said) many spe-
cially valuable aspects of that same enlightenment."[6] The ubiquity
of belief in the reality of demons and of magic can hardly be over-
stressed. It was not confined to a particular social class and was not
the characteristic of one region or one epoch or one system of religious belief. Magic not only resolved difficulties, but also provided an explanation for them. In the words of Peter Brown: "For
pagan and Christian alike, misfortune was unambiguously the
work of suprahuman agents, the *daemons*. Whether these were the
ambivalent 'spirits of the lower air' of much pagan belief, or ac-
tively hostile to the human race, as in Zoroastrianism, Christianity
and the Gnostic sects, demons were the effective agents of all misfortune. The sorcerer caused misfortune only by manipulating the
demons, the curser by 'delivering over' his victim to their hostility."[7] When the apocryphal Acts report exorcisms of demons
and even apostolic conversations with demons, they reflect the general world view of antiquity.

Reports from patristic literature indicate that Christians indulged
in charismatic activities akin to magic even though they used the
term "magic" almost without exception as a term of social disapproval, presuming that magic was done by enemies and miracles by
themselves. Christians had no doubt that they or their fellow
Christians could and did do such things as cast out demons, raise
the "dead," and heal the sick through supernatural power. They
took pride in this capacity and the intellectuals among them found
it a valuable apologetic device. Demons, those world-filling causers
of misfortune, could be exorcised by Christians far more effectively
than by pagans in the opinion of Justin:

6. MacMullen, *Enemies of the Roman Order*, p. 126.
7. Brown, *Religion and Society in the Age of St. Augustine*, p. 131.

For every demon, when exorcised in the name of this very Son of God who is the First-born of every creature, who became man by the Virgin, who suffered, and was crucified under Pontius Pilate by your nation, who died, who rose from the dead and ascended into heaven, is overcome and subdued. But though you exorcise any demon in the name of any of those who were among you—either kings, or righteous men, or prophets, or patriarchs—it will not be subject to you. But if any of you exorcise it in the God of Abraham, and the God of Isaac, and the God of Jacob it will perhaps be subject to you.[8]

Clearly, charismatic action, or magic, was honored by Justin and the other Christians of his time. In a world filled with demons the charismatic power of Christians undoubtedly made a strong impact, especially on those who were too economically or socially dispossessed to afford magicians or to use magic confidently themselves.

In his Second Apology, directed to the Roman Senate, Justin assumes that the Christians' capabilities would awe even that august body.

But "Jesus" his name as man and Savior, has also significance. For he was made man also, as we before said, having been conceived according to the will of God the Father, for the sake of believing men, and for the destruction of the demons. And now you can learn this from what is under your own observation. For numberless demoniacs throughout the whole world, and in your city, many of our Christian men exorcising them in the name of Jesus Christ, who was crucified under Pontius Pilate, have healed and do heal, rendering helpless and driving the possessing devil out of the men, though they could not be cured by all the other exorcists, and those who used incantations and drugs.[9]

Justin appeals directly and confidently here to the evidence of charismatic activities as validation for his theological arguments.

In his own Apology, Tertullian uses the same kind of example to buttress his arguments. He says that a possessed person who is "bidden to speak by a follower of Christ will readily make the truthful confession that he is a demon, as elsewhere he has falsely

8. Justin *Dialogue with Trypho* 85.
9. Justin *Apology* 6.

asserted that he is a god."[10] Indeed, for Tertullian, the power of the prayers of Christians can "extort the rains of heaven, recall the souls of the departed from the very path of death, transform the weak, restore the sick, purge the possessed, open prison bars, loose the bonds of the innocent."[11] Far from denying the necessity of supernatural remedies, Christians argued that their powers in that regard were superior to those of any other persons.

It is significant that both Justin and Tertullian use the argument from charismatic power in their apologies. This argument was apparently common in the early church, for Origen does the same. He cites the number of cases of cures and exorcisms due to the name and history of Jesus as evidence on his side in his argument with Celsus, an argument destined for an audience probably not composed entirely of philosophically minded Christians.[12]

There is evidence that some Christians of the second century thought that the dead could be raised by charismatic Christians. Irenaeus, who knows of several such events, reports that opponents of orthodoxy do not raise the dead. "So far are they from being able to raise the dead, as the Lord raised them and the apostles did by means of prayer and as has been done *frequently* in the brotherhood on account of some necessity—the entire church in that particular locality entreating with much fasting and prayer, the spirit of the dead man has returned and he has been bestowed in answer to the prayers of the saints—that they do not even believe that this can possibly be done."[13] (emphasis added) Referring again to the raising of dead persons, Irenaeus says: "Some do certainly and truly drive out devils, so that those who have thus been cleansed from evil spirits both believe and join themselves to the church. Others have foreknowledge of things to come; they see visions, and utter prophetic expressions. Others still heal the sick by laying their hands upon them, and they are made whole. Yea, moreover, as I have said, the dead even have been raised up and remained among us for many years."[14] From the evidence of these passages we know that Irenaeus himself assumed that raising the dead was a ca-

10. Tertullian *Apologeticus* 23.
11. Tertullian *de Orat.* 29.
12. Cf. Origen, *Contra Celsum* 1.6, 1.46, 3.24.
13. Irenaeus *Adversus Haereses* 2.31.
14. Irenaeus *Adversus Haereses* 2.32.

pacity of charismatically gifted Christians. Furthermore, Irenaeus provides additional evidence that one of the means by which Christians sought to convert pagans was the effective use of charismatic power. Irenaeus is writing about the Christians living in settled communities, but the powers he attributes to members of the church accord remarkably well with the powers the Acts attribute to apostles.

Irenaeus, Tertullian, Origen, and Justin were learned men who, nevertheless, lived in a social world founded on belief in miracle and magic and charismatic power. What was true for them was also true for simple Christians. The apostles in the apocryphal Acts are reported to heal the sick by prayer and the name of Jesus, to raise the dead, to cast out and converse with demons. In the context of their time this is not material wholly in the realm of fantasy but fiction modeled on common second-century beliefs about the world. By looking carefully at this fiction, we can come to a fuller understanding of the world view on which it was based and of the people who composed and enjoyed it.

Like the authors of the apocryphal Acts, Origen believed that the apostles of the first century were capable of "miracles and wonders" greater than those possible in his own day. He compared his conception of the apostles' capabilities to the lesser capabilities of persons with whom he was acquainted. In *Contra Celsum* he writes that "without miracles and wonders they [the apostles] would not have persuaded those who heard new doctrines and new teaching to leave their traditional religion and to accept the apostles' teachings at the risk of their lives. Traces of that Holy Spirit who appeared in the form of a dove are still preserved among Christians. They charm demons away and perform many cures and perceive certain things about the future according to the will of the Logos." [15] Origen is not content simply to state that such remarkable things happen, but has considered the technology of magic quite carefully. Through his writings we can gain some understanding both of his general theory of magic and of the specific techniques he knew to be employed in Christian magic.

Origen does not believe that Christians enjoy a monopoly in the efficacious use of magical phrases or divine names:

15. Origen *Contra Celsum* 1.46.

If, then, we shall be able to establish . . . the nature of powerful names, some of which are used by the learned amongst the Egyptians, or by the magi among the Persians, and by the Indian philosophers called Brahmans, or by the Samanaeans, and others in different countries; and shall be able to make out that the so-called magic is not, as the followers of Epicurus and Aristotle suppose, an altogether uncertain thing but is, as those skilled in it prove, a consistent system, having words which are known to exceedingly few; then we say that the names Sabaoth and Adonai, and the other names treated with so much reverence among the Hebrews, are not applicable to any ordinary created thing but belong to a secret theology which refers to the Framer of all things. These names, accordingly, when pronounced with that attendant train of circumstances which is appropriate to their nature, are possessed of great power.[16]

To understand the method of Christian magic we must understand what Origen might have meant by "that attendant train of circumstances which is appropriate."

One factor of crucial importance is that the names be pronounced in their original language:

If we were to translate the name Israel into Greek or another language we would effect nothing. But if we keep it as it is, linking it onto those words with which experts in these matters have thought fit to connect it, then something would happen in accordance with the power which such invocations are said to possess when a formula of this kind is pronounced. We would say the same also of the word Sabaoth, which is frequently used in spells because if we translate the name into "Lord of the powers" or "Lord of hosts" or "almighty" (for its interpreters explain it differently) we would effect nothing; whereas if we keep it with its own sounds, we will cause something to happen, according to the opinion of experts in these matters.[17]

Origen retains the Hebrew names of God for Christian use, but he adds another name. "And a similar philosophy of names applies

16. Origen *Contra Celsum* 1.24.
17. Origen *Contra Celsum* 5.45; see also Adolf Jensen who writes that "magic is related to the religious world view as applied physics is related to theoretical physics; nothing prevents a great technician from being a great theoretician also" (*Myth and Cult among Primitive Peoples*, p. 231).

also to our Jesus, whose name has already been seen, in an unmistakable manner, to have expelled myriads of evil spirits from the souls and bodies of men so great was the power which it exerted upon those from whom the spirits were driven out." [18] The theory of names Origen holds is that the very sound of the name has inherent power. But the name itself apparently needs to be used in conjunction with a "train of circumstances" and words which experts think should be connected to it.

The name of Jesus is not used in isolation by Christians. They "do not get the power which they seem to possess by any incantations but by the name of Jesus with the recital of the histories about him. For when these are pronounced they have often made demons to be driven out of men and especially when those who utter them speak with real sincerity and real belief. In fact the name of Jesus is so powerful against the demons that sometimes it is effective even when pronounced by bad men. . . . It is clear that Christians make no use of spells but only of the name of Jesus with other words which are believed to be effective, taken from divine scripture." [19] The words connected with the name of Jesus include "histories" about Jesus and selections from Scripture believed effective. Such selections were probably reports of the mighty power of God and instances of the successful resolution of particular problems.

Origen was convinced by personal experience that the magical phrases uttered by Christians were effective. In telling us of this conviction he mentions another factor common in Christian magical practice.

There is an untold number of both Greeks and barbarians who believe in Jesus. Some display evidence of having received some miraculous power because of this faith, shown in the people whom they cure; upon those who need healing they use no other invocation than that of the supreme God and of the name of Jesus together with the history about him. By these we also have seen many delivered from serious ailments, and from mental distraction and madness, and countless other diseases which neither men nor demons had cured. [20]

18. Origen *Contra Celsum* 1.25.
19. Origen *Contra Celsum* 1.6.
20. Origen *Contra Celsum* 3.24.

For the first time Origen's respect for the Hebrew names of God can be coupled with his respect for the name of Jesus, for he advocates invocation of the supreme God. We are capable of sketching a framework for the sorts of formulas with which Origen was familiar in Christian magical practice. The formulas had at least four component parts:

1. Invocation of the Supreme God. Judging by Origen's great respect for the names Sabaoth and Adonai (when untranslated and properly pronounced), the invocations often had these names as essential elements.
2. Recital of relevant or powerful sections of holy scripture, probably from both the Old and New Testaments.
3. Pronunciation of the name of Jesus.
4. Recitation of a "history" of Jesus.

Origen does not tell us what a "history" of Jesus might be like, but Justin seems to do so in his Dialogue with Trypho. There Justin quotes an exorcism formula in which the following is an integral part. The Son of God is "the First-born of every creature, who became man by the Virgin, who suffered, and was crucified under Pontius Pilate . . . , who died, who rose from the dead and ascended into heaven." [21] If this sort of formula is what Origen meant by a "history," then "histories" are the Christian message in synopsis. By combining our knowledge that Christians used their magical or charismatic phrases as apologetic devices intended to prove the truth of the faith with the knowledge that their healing techniques seem to have contained synopses of Christian teachings, we can see that the teaching function and the healing/exorcising function were to some extent identical from at least the period of Justin to the period of Origen. Those pagans who were healed by Christians—and they are confidently and repeatedly claimed by our sources to have been legion—were at the same time, by the same act, made cognizant of the basic facts of the faith. The apostles described in the Acts need not have taught and then healed, or have healed and then taught. Healing taught; teaching healed.

A similar process appears in the writing of Irenaeus when he argues from charismatic efficacy for the truth of Christian preaching. "If, therefore, the name of our Lord Jesus Christ even now confers

21. Justin *Dialogue with Trypho* 85.

benefits, and cures thoroughly and effectively all who anywhere believe on Him, but not that of Simon or Menander, or Carpocrates, or of any other man whatever, it is manifest that, when he was made man, he held fellowship with his own creation and did all things truly through the power of God according to the will of the Father of all, as the prophets foretold." [22] From the evidence in Justin and Origen about the efficacy of "histories," it seems reasonable to conclude that Irenaeus is not arguing that because cures work in Jesus' name propositions of the faith are true, but that because those propositions were enunciated in the act of healing itself their truth was demonstrated by their efficacy. The phrase "name of Jesus" might then imply not only the word "Jesus" but also phrases descriptive of Jesus' cosmic and salvific career, that is, "histories."

We find similar "histories" in the apocryphal Acts. In a fabulous tale where John attempts to reknit some fragmented precious stones, he says:

Lord Jesus Christ, unto whom nothing is impossible, who when the world was broken by the tree of concupiscence didst restore it again in thy faithfulness by the tree of the cross, who didst give to one born blind the eyes which nature had denied him, who didst recall Lazarus, dead and buried, after the fourth day unto the light; and has subjected all diseases and all sicknesses unto the word of they power; so also now do with these precious stones . . . recover thou them, Lord, now by the hands of thine angels, that by their value the work of mercy may be fulfilled, and make these men believe in thee the unbegotten father through thine only-begotten Son Jesus Christ our Lord (A.Jn. 14, James).

Here the use of a "history" has the required result. The stones are mended and an unbeliever, "Craton, the philosopher, with his disciples, seeing this, fell at the feet of the apostle and believed" (A.Jn. 14, James).

A passage in the Acts of Thomas shows that the distinction between a healing and simple preaching (with selections drawn from holy scripture) was not clearly defined. The apostle, given the task of raising up a young girl, lays his hand on her head and says:

22. Irenaeus *Adversus Haereses* 2.32.

Jesus, who dost appear to us at all times—for this is thy will, that we should ever seek thee, and thou thyself hast given us this right to ask and to receive, and not only didst thou grant this, but also thou didst teach us to pray,—thou who art not seen with our bodily eyes, but art never hidden at all from those of our soul, and in thy form indeed art hidden, but in thy works art manifest to us; and by thy many works we have come to know thee, as we are able, but thou thyself hast given to us thy gifts without measure, saying: *Ask, and it shall be given you, seek and ye shall find, knock and it shall be opened unto you* (A.Th. 6:53).

This passage continues on for some length in the same vein. The girl is raised successfully. We can see that the functions of preaching and charismatic healing are inseparably fused. Reports of the kind of activities and procedures engaged in by apostles in the apocryphal Acts are in accord with Christian practice in the late second century.

The "histories" apparently used in exorcism seem to have been somewhat like creeds, the phrases spoken at baptism. In the early church, baptism involved a renunciation of Satan and was thought to seal new Christians from future demonic influence. It is possible that creedal formulas and exorcism formulas were closely related and that for the common people, at least, baptism was seen to be exorcism raised to a peak of efficacy. J. N. D. Kelly writes, in *Early Christian Creeds*, that creeds appeared in numerous contexts in the early church and that, "the exorcism of devils was widely practiced in the early Church, and the codification of suitable formulae of proved potency seems to have set in fairly soon."[23] He points out, in fact, that a creedlike exorcism formula appears in as early a source as the Acts of the Apostles, "thus St. Peter (Acts 3, 6) cured the lame man at Beautiful Gate by solemnly adjuring him, 'In the name of Jesus Christ, the Nazoraean, walk.' A little later, when asked to explain the miracle (4, 10), he elaborates the formula into 'in the name of Jesus Christ, the Nazoraean, Whom you crucified, Whom God raised from the dead.'"[24]

To ensure effective baptism and effective exorcism there would

23. Kelly, *Early Christian Creeds*, p. 14.
24. Ibid., p. 19.

have been concern within the early church that the creed or "history" be precisely right. An inaccurate "history" would be ineffective. Origen and other Christians were aware of the magical power of words. It should not be surprising to find that the apocryphal Acts take such power for granted.

III

The Apostles

THE APOCRYPHAL ACTS feature men called apostles, itinerant Christian preachers who live in poverty and are often credited with miraculous power to heal. While the Acts are set in the first century, apostles continued to exist into the second century as a class of Christian person. The Didache, from the mid-second century or earlier, reflects a time when the church found apostles to be so common as to offer a threat to church order.[1] It contains strict regulations for the reception of apostles. "But in regard to the apostles and prophets, according to the ordinance of the gospel, so do ye. And every apostle who cometh to you, let him be received as the Lord; but he shall not remain more than one day; if, however, there be need, then the next day; but if he remain three days, he is a false prophet. But when the apostle departeth, let him take nothing except bread enough till he lodge again; but if he ask money he is a false prophet."[2] Second-century apostles seem to have been viewed with considerable suspicion by church officials. John Gager, writing in reference to Didache 15, says that the passage would seem to imply that the congregation accorded greater authority to wandering prophets and apostles than to local functionaries.[3]

1. Didache 11.
2. Didache 11.
3. Gager, *Kingdom and Community*, p. 73; see also Adolf von Harnack, *The Mis-*

Origen of Alexandria is familiar with men who were like apostles, although he does not use that term. He writes that some Christians "have done the work of going round not only cities but even villages and country cottages to make others also pious toward God. One could not say that they did this for the sake of wealth, since sometimes they do not even accept money for the necessities of life."[4] Itinerant Christian preachers were still prevalent in the early third century, judging from this passage.

References to contemporary apostles disappear from orthodox writings after the Didache. As the church became more stable and a firm church hierarchy began to form (a process well under way by circa 113, as is evident in Ignatius's letters), many itinerant Christian preachers beholden to no one but God were thought of as "heretics" spreading not the Gospel but false doctrine. Throughout this study we shall use the term "apostle" to refer to these "itinerant, charismatic, wonder-working Christian preachers." At times, officials of the established church may have called such men false apostles (and we may infer from this that they called themselves "apostles"), but it is of no particular importance to this study what they were called in the later second century. The relationship of such men to their audiences is our concern.

The apocryphal Acts were written by second- and early third-century Christians who had known the apostles of their time, encountered them in their towns, and listened to their preaching. They may even have been healed by their ministrations.

The disappearance of apostles as acceptable Christian functionaries in the later second century might have stimulated the production of apocryphal Acts. Some Christians may have sought to preserve in narrative form a style of Christian ministry vanishing from the world. If so, then the social conditions reflected in the Acts would have been those remembered from a period slightly earlier than that of the Acts' composition.

We know little or nothing about the apostles, or wandering Christian wonder-workers, of the second century. From the apoc-

---

sion and Expansion of Christianity in the First Three Centuries. Harnack is confident that apostles existed in the second century and regrets that we know little about them (pp. 349, 351). Also see Gerd Theissen, *Sociology of Early Palestinian Christianity*.

4. Origen *Contra Celsum* 3.9.

ryphal Acts we can, perhaps, learn how they were viewed by persons who respected or revered them, but this evidence can at best lead us to assess probabilities rather than to draw firm conclusions. The antiheretical writers permit us glimpses of itinerant Christian preachers, but their writings are as veiled by contempt as the apocryphal Acts are by hyperbole. Nevertheless, the greater part of the spread of Christianity probably came about through the efforts of itinerant wonder-workers rather than by the efforts of high-minded thinkers writing to an elite.

In order to investigate the social world of the community behind the Acts, we must first look at the apostles, the itinerant leaders those people revered. Apostolic leadership is best characterized as charismatic. Max Weber has said that many social movements begin with leadership based on charisma, evident and exceptional gifts; but that, if they are to endure, such movements must undergo the process of the routinization of charisma into an hierarchically organized, self-sustaining social system.[5] In a passage relevant to the characteristics of the apostles and the community behind the Acts, Weber theorizes:

Charisma knows only inner determination and inner restraint. The holder of charisma seizes the task that is adequate for him and demands obedience and a following by virtue of his mission. His success determines whether he finds them. His charismatic claim breaks down if his mission is not recognized by those to whom he feels he has been sent. If they recognize him he is their master—so long as he knows how to maintain recognition through "proving" himself. But he does not derive his "right" from their will, in the manner of an election. Rather, the reverse holds: it is the duty of those to whom he addresses his mission to recognize him as their charismatic leader.[6]

The apostle in the Acts is such a charismatic leader, one who has no discernible ties to any structured church. His legitimacy does not come from office but from his personal power to transform onlookers into adherents. Robert Tucker defines the charismatic

5. Weber, *From Max Weber: Essays in Sociology*, ed. and trans. H. H. Garth and C. Mills, p. 297.
6. Ibid., pp. 246–47.

leader in particularly religious terms and shows that the miracle-working activities of apostles are in keeping with their social role as charismatic leaders.

The charismatic leader is one in whom, by virtue of unusual personal qualities, the promise or hope of salvation—deliverance from distress—appears to be embodied. He is a leader who convincingly offers himself to a group of people in distress as one peculiarly qualified to lead them out of their predicament. He is in essence a savior, or one who is so perceived by his followers. *Charismatic leadership is specifically salvationist or messianic in nature.* Herein lies its distinctiveness in relation to such broader and more nebulous categories as "inspired leadership" or "heroic leadership." Furthermore, this fundamental characteristic of charismatic leadership helps to explain the special emotional intensity of the charismatic response, and also why the sustaining of charisma requires the leader to furnish periodical "proof" of the powers that he claims. (Tucker's emphasis)[7]

The apocryphal Acts are hyperbolic collections of the "proofs" reportedly offered by charismatic apostles and of reports that people found those "proofs" convincing. The apostles were more than simple magicians. They carried a Christian message and they embodied, in their life-style and preaching, certain heroic virtues.

Three of the apostles' heroic virtues are chastity, endurance, and freedom from structured social obligations. These three virtues are closely related, in that each shows the apostles to have been largely asocial beings. They tell us about the values and way of living both of the charismatic leaders who may have visited the community behind the Acts and of the individuals within the community that composed the Acts. We will discuss each separately.

The Acts demand absolute sexual continence, with celibacy urged on those not married and a suspension of marital relations on persons married. One of the most savage attacks on the institution of marriage is found in the Acts of John, as quoted in the apocryphal Epistle of Titus; marriage is said to be "a device of the serpent, a disregard of the teaching, an injury to the seed, a gift of death, a work of destruction, a teaching of division, a work of cor-

7. Tucker, "The Theory of Charismatic Action," *Daedalus* 97(1968):742–43.

ruption, etc."[8] In the Acts of Paul the beatitudes are transformed to read, in part,

Blessed are they who have kept the flesh pure, for they shall become a temple of God.
Blessed are the continent, for to them will God speak.

Blessed are the bodies of the virgins, for they shall be well pleasing to God, and shall not lose the reward of their purity. For the word of the Father shall be for them a work of salvation in the day of his Son, and they shall have rest for ever and ever (A.Pl. 3:5–6).

The other Acts are no different, stressing continence in discourses and holding up as exemplars of piety women (and occasionally men) who become Christians and renounce their marital sexual relationships (e.g., A.An. 5 and A.Pt. 9:34). As for the notion that intercourse ought to be condoned if only to produce children, Thomas says:

If you abandon this filthy intercourse you become holy temples, pure and free from afflictions and pains both manifest and hidden, and you will not be girt about with cares for life and for children, the end of which is destruction. But if you get many children, then for their sakes you become robbers and avaricious, (people who) flay orphans and defraud widows, and by so doing you subject yourselves to the most grievous punishments. For the majority of children become unprofitable, possessed by demons, some openly and some in secret; for they become either lunatic or half-withered (consumptive) or crippled or deaf or dumb or paralytic or stupid. Even if they are healthy, again will they be unserviceable, performing useless and abominable deeds; for they are caught either in adultery or in murder or in theft or in unchastity, and by all these you will be afflicted (A.Th. 1:12).

Such an outburst could be appreciated by a deeply alienated community, one shut off from the normal life of society in the ancient world.

The absolute chastity demanded in the Acts requires the end of

8. Schneemelcher and Hennecke, eds., *New Testament Apocrypha*, pp. 209–10.

family life in the sense of an end to reproduction. It leads to the collapse of established marriages (except in the unusual instances of converted married couples) and even to an end to cordiality between parents and converted children. In the Acts of Paul for instance, Thecla's own mother demands that her daughter be executed because of her determined celibacy (A.Pl. 3:20). The familial discord hyperbolized in that story might be expected in any society following the conversion of children or spouses to a strange and continent cult.

The apostle's virtue of endurance is best seen in his capacity to endure torture and imprisonment. Peter, while hanging from the cross, delivers a lengthy discourse on the symbolism of his plight (A.Pt. 9:38). Andrew does the same, even going so far as to plead with the worried proconsul not to release him (A.An. Narr. 34). Paul and Thomas have no difficulty with imprisonment, setting themselves free and incarcerating themselves again at will (A.Pl. 7 and A.Th. 13:154). In the Acts of Paul, Thecla goes through a myriad of tortures without suffering any damage (A.Pl. 3:21–38). Such endurance implicitly presumes the injustice and even the illegitimacy of judicial authority. The enduring apostle is ideally free from being affected by the coercive pressures applied by the judiciary and, in being free, he can oppose authority with impunity.

The apostle's freedom to oppose the normal social order denies to the established authorities moral right to uphold that order, for it is God's will that the apostle be immune to judicial pressure. The apostle is set up as a rival to proconsuls, high priests, and kings. Indeed, he represents opposition to any established authority, be it religious, imperial, or local. In his opposition to families the apostle represents opposition to the *sine qua non* of social life; in his opposition to figures of authority he represents opposition to social control.

The virtue of freedom from structured social obligations is one with several aspects. The apostle disdains wealth, distributing whatever he has to the poor. John says, disapprovingly, that in order to obtain money people must "guard their houses against thieves, till their estates, ply the plough, pay taxes, build storehouses, strive for gain, try to baffle the attacks of the strong, etc." (A.Jn. 16, James). Not only wealth, then, but also the productive activity essential to social life ought to be condemned. The apostle's virtue in renouncing wealth seems not to stem as much from the intention to enable the poor to become economically secure as from an adamant struggle to remain poor himself. The Acts of Andrew, apparently, once contained a story of a son converted to Christianity whose parents, to spite him, "left all their money to public uses" (A.An. 12, James). The son reacquired their property and "spent his income on the poor" (A.An. 12, James). Here the power of the state even to serve the community is disvalued in favor of a general dispersal of funds.

The apostle does not represent antique republicanism in rebellion against the empire, nor does he represent Christian communism (which is a form of ownership and not an adamant refusal to own). No apostle has obligations to any town, city, state, or kingdom. He is always itinerant, always on the move with his destinations determined for him by dreams and visions. No apostle has an occupation, with the possible exception of Thomas (an architect who builds in heaven and not on earth). Virtue stems from freedom from the entanglements of social life. A passage in the Acts of Thomas mentions that the following things should be given up: homes, possessions, fathers, mothers, fosters, bodily consorts, children (A.Th. 6:61). While the apostles and their followers renounce fine clothing and fast frequently, the renunciations that are stressed in the Acts are social, familial, and marital.

The apostles are not portrayed as opposed to Rome per se; Thomas in India possesses the same virtues as apostles in Mediterranean lands. The virtue of the apostle lies in his opposition not to Rome but to social life in general and in the concomitant capacity for self-control that enabled such an asocial existence to be endured. This idea is in accord with Weber's idea of the charismatic leader. "Genuine charismatic domination, therefore, knows of no abstract legal codes and statutes and of no 'formal' way of adjudication. Its 'objective' law emanates concretely from the highly personal experience of heavenly grace and from the god-like strength of the hero. Charismatic domination means a rejection of all ties to any external order in favor of the exclusive glorification of the genuine mentality of the prophet and hero. Hence, its attitude is revolutionary and transvalues everything; it makes a sovereign break with all traditional or rational norms."[9] The apostle in the apocryphal Acts possesses these characteristics of the charismatic leader and, in embodying his own peculiar authority, he and his adherents break free from all other authority.

However asocial, the apostle is moral in the sense of disapproving of such deeds as theft, murder, adultery, and revenge. He does not oppose moral order but social structure. Implicitly, the more continent, enduring, and free from social obligations an individual is, the more moral he will be.

The apostle exists and functions to convert others to Christianity, not merely to advocate social dissolution. Here lies a problem. In some fashion those he converts must band together, for Christianity is a religion focused on a community of believers. This focus is evident in the Acts in that all ritual activity occurs in a group context. There is a tension here, a conflict between the asocial ideal embodied in the apostle himself and the Christian end the apostle functions to attain. The Christian social structure that emerges at least partially because of the activities of apostles will have to be one which to some extent rejects the asocial virtues of apostles and, therefore, disowns the apostles themselves. The Didache, as we have seen, shows evidence of this process. There, apostles are implicitly disvalued in that their presence in the church community is required to be as brief as possible. In the Acts apostles find both rejection and support. In the following section of this study we shall examine the kinds of responses apostles received as reported in the apocryphal Acts.

Fundamentally the apostle has significant relationships with two classes of people: those who oppose him and his mission and those who accept him and his mission. In the first category figures of authority and husbands of newly continent Christian wives predominate. In the second category are those he converts and those who accept him as a legitimate apostle. We will first examine the relationship between the apostle and his opponents with reference to the sorcery accusations they lodge against him. Then we will turn to an examination of the complex relationship between the apostle and those he converts.

Sorcery accusations are common in the apocryphal Acts. On the

---

9. Weber, *Essays in Sociology*, p. 250.

surface they appear to be simple matters. The apostle comes to town and performs charismatic actions that result in the conversion of a number of people. These people decide to live a continent life and the enemies of the apostle accuse him of being a sorcerer. We might presume that since Roman law prohibited sorcery the enemies of the apostle would define his charismatic actions as criminal. In fact, the asocial virtues of the apostle are the most usual cause of sorcery accusations. We shall examine several sorcery accusations reported in the Acts in order to demonstrate this common theme.

In a rather fragmentary portion of the Acts of Paul the apostle delivers a discourse against the gods of Ephesus (A.Pl. 7). Paul is condemned to be executed. Diophantes, a freedman of the governor, reflects on the fact that his wife has become continent and spends her time with Paul. He becomes jealous and hastens the conflict of Paul and the beasts. Eventually the wife of the governor is also converted to a life of sexual continence, and the governor plans the execution of Paul "partly because of his suspicion against his wife, partly because he (Paul) had not fled" (A.Pl. 7). A lion is set loose on Paul and there is the cry "Away with the sorcerer!" (A.Pl. 7). Paul's attacks on the gods, his encouragement of continence for converted wives, his refusal to flee (e.g., his willingness to endure imprisonment and execution) lead to an accusation of sorcery. We would expect to find his charismatic activities cited in this episode of trial but none are mentioned.

Something similar occurs in the well-preserved Thecla story in the same Acts (A.Pl. 3). Paul converts a substantial percentage of the women of Iconium to a life of continence. At the urging of two Christian heretics he is brought to the governor by Thecla's betrothed, who tells the governor "this man—we know now whence he is—who does not allow maidens to marry, let him declare before thee for what cause he teaches these things" (A.Pl. 3:15). Paul preaches briefly to the governor and is remanded for later attention. When brought forward later Paul hears the crowd shout "He is a sorcerer! Away with him!" (A.Pl. 3:20). Again, charges are not based on laws against sorcery but rather derive from the apostle's advocacy of continence. The people, nevertheless, voice an accusation of sorcery. It is significant that in both of these cases the accusations come from the masses, not from the judges.

The Acts of Thomas has the greatest number of accusations of sorcery, which for the most part fall into the pattern we have seen forming. Thomas convinces a newly married pair to remain continent; the bride's father calls him a sorcerer (A.Th. 1:16).

Toward the end of the Acts Thomas converts two royal women to a life of continence, and their husbands repeatedly accuse him of sorcery for that reason (A.Th. 10:130, 11:134, passim). Ultimately the two husbands have Thomas executed.

One accusation of sorcery in the Acts of Thomas is related to charismatic activities. People say that Thomas gives to the poor, teaches of a new God, heals the sick, drives out devils and does many other wonderful things and that "we think he is a magician." Yet their accusation is immediately tempered; "But his works of compassion, and the healings which are wrought by him without reward, and moreover his simplicity and kindness and the quality of his faith show that he is righteous. . . ." (A.Th. 2:20) The accusation here, like those in the Acts of Paul, stems from the masses.

Another accusation related both to the apostle's virtues and to his charismatic power can be found in the Acts of Thomas. Jailers who ineffectually guard Thomas ask, "What sin have we committed against that sorcerer . . . ?" They go on to say that through his power Thomas opened the prison doors, and all the prisoners might have escaped. The guards go to the king and ask him to "release that sorcerer, or commend him to be kept in custody somewhere else" (A.Th. 13:162). In this instance Thomas's freedom from coercive power is his sorcery.

We have identified the three virtues that define the apostle as an exemplary, if asocial, figure: his continence, his endurance, his freedom from social obligations. Accusations of sorcery in the apocryphal Acts commonly focus on these virtues as possessed by the apostle or as adopted by his followers. The apostle is often accused of sorcery for converting married women to sexual continence and thus breaking up families and alienating husbands. His capacity to walk freely from prison, his outspokenness against traditional styles of religion, and his generosity toward the poor lead to accusations of sorcery. These accusations are almost entirely social in nature and have hardly anything at all to do with conflicting notions of miracle and magic.

The word sorcery does seem to imply magic. In an article on the apocryphal Acts, Paul Achtemeier writes that magic and sorcery were quite at home in the Hellenistic world of the apocryphal Acts. He states that, "It is no wonder, therefore, that accusations are raised both against Christ's followers and by them against others. The same rule seems to apply which we observed earlier, namely, one's own deeds are by God's power, those of others by magic." [10] Achtemeier's assumption is that a charge of sorcery stems from the notion that the apostles were doing criminal magic. This is not the case; the apostles are usually called sorcerers because they are, in the eyes of their opponents, asocial and outside the normal structures of society. In understanding this odd fact we will apprehend something of the social reality behind the apocryphal Acts.

In anthropology, witchcraft and sorcery accusations are seriously considered. Except for a certain gender bias, the terms witchcraft and sorcery are synonymous in their sense as accusations. Mary Douglas writes of witchcraft accusations in *Purity and Danger* that:

> It is the existence of an angry person in an interstitial position which is dangerous, . . . When such unhappy or angry persons are accused of witchcraft it is like a warning . . . a means of exerting control. . . . Witchcraft, then, is found in nonstructure. [11]

Her theory fits the situation in the apocryphal Acts, especially if we understand the apostles to be charismatic leaders in a sociological sense: persons possessed of unstructured personal power. The itinerant Christian wonder-worker who has the virtues credited to the apostles must necessarily be difficult to control; his endurance renders him virtually beyond punishment. He certainly has rebellious intentions and these intentions are entirely indefinite. His virtues combined with his charismatic capacities credit him with "antisocial psychic power." By no means does he fit into the social structure of the ancient world; he embodies no articulated, competitive social order, and yet he preaches the inadequacy of the present system of society. It is not odd that sorcery accusations are only tenuously related to charges that the apostles were doing magic.

10. Achtemeier, "Jesus and the Disciples as Miracle Workers in the Apocryphal New Testament," in *Aspects of Religious Propaganda in Judaism and Early Christianity*, ed. Elisabeth Schüssler Fiorenza, p. 168.

11. Douglas, *Purity and Danger*, p. 102.

This relationship is in accord with what we should expect from conflict between asocial and charismatic figures and the representatives of social order.

In *Witchcraft* Lucy Mair discusses the theory that witchcraft accusations aid in establishing social norms by defining what is outside social acceptability: "Generalizations about witches assert, by condemning their opposite, the values of the society where the assertion is being made, and to this extent the belief makes its contribution to maintenance of social order."[12] Like Douglas, she finds that an accusation of witchcraft or sorcery points to a person outside the normal structure of society, either someone who does not have a set place in that society or someone who is within it but challenging its norms.

The theory Mair presents is remarkably similar to the theory of the social function of heresy accusations Samuel Laeuchli develops in his book *The Serpent and the Dove*. Therein he contends that, in the history of the Christian Church, heresy accusations were a primary means by which the church defined its own beliefs. By defining what was wrong, heresy accusations brought about the definition of what was correct. Through the conflict with heresy (or by the device of heresy accusations), the church clarified its own thinking. An accusation of heresy is, in a sense, equivalent on the religious level to an accusation of witchcraft or sorcery on the social level.

In the story of Paul and Thecla Paul is brought before the governor by two Christian heretics and by Thecla's aggrieved betrothed in the company of Thecla's outraged mother (A.Pl. 3:20). An accusation of sorcery by the crowd soon follows. As heresy accusa-

---

12. Mair, *Witchcraft*, p. 203. Maxwell Marwick sees sorcery (and witchcraft) as a "conservative force."

This view implies that beliefs in sorcery afford the means, not merely to preserving the general shape and the periodic rhythms of a society in a relatively unchanging environment, but also of increasing its resistance to outside influences. . . . rapid social changes are likely to cause an increased preoccupation with beliefs in sorcery and witchcraft. *A priori*, this would seem to be true whether we approach the problem either in terms of changes in the values defining the ideal conduct or in terms of the dynamics of social relationships. This is because one of the effects of social change is to bring new values and norms into conflict with indigenous ones; and another is the creation of new relationships and the fundamental modification of old ones (*Sorcery in Its Social Setting*, pp. 247–48).

tions seem to be a religious transformation of social sorcery accusations, Paul is doubly culpable; he is heretical in the eyes of the two Christians and asocial in the eyes of those who regret that Thecla will not marry.

A similar link between sorcery and heresy can be found in the Acts of Peter when Peter is accused *in absentia* of being a sorcerer by followers of Simon Magus (A.Pt. 2:4). In turn, Simon Magus is accused by Peter of being both a sorcerer and a heretic (see especially A.Pt. 6:17, 8:23). Simon is a sorcerer because his claim to legitimate authority undermines the authority of Peter. In a group following charismatically legitimized leadership, the presence of a rival charismatic leader must be considered as a threat to legitimate authority made by someone within the society (e.g., recognizing and asserting Christian charismatic leadership) who is opposed to the norms of the society (in this instance the normative authority of Peter). Since Simon does have charisma, he cannot be controlled by normal means. If Simon is to be controlled, he must be defeated in a contest to determine who possesses the greater charisma; and this happens in the Acts of Peter (A.Pt. 5:12, 8:28–29). Further, the legitimacy of his charisma must be denied. This is the function of the sorcery accusations leveled against him by Peter; his power is said to come from the devil (A.Pt. 2:5) and not from God. Simon's intellectual disagreements with Peter make of him a heretic, a sorcerer on the level of doctrine. Simon's charismatic actions and, presumably, ritual activities are repeatedly accused of being "magic" (A.Pt. 2:6, 6:16, 6:17).

Irenaeus reports that a Christian teacher, apparently charismatically gifted, arrived in Lyons and won many adherents away from Irenaeus's church. This teacher, Marcus, is accused by Irenaeus of being "a perfect adept in magical impostures," and he is included in Irenaeus' catalog of heretics.[13] Marcus's intellectual dissent makes him a heretic; his challenge to the church order dominated by Irenaeus (a church order into which he claims to fit, but in which Irenaeus finds no place for him) leads Irenaeus to call him a magician. Irenaeus devotes a chapter to taking his own accusations seriously, endeavoring to prove his adversary's rituals to be magic and, therefore, illegitimate. In general we find that an accusation of

13. Irenaeus *Adversus Haereses* 1.13ff.

sorcery on the social level, an accusation of heresy on the level of doctrine, and an accusation of magic on the level of ritual are simple transformations of the same thing: a denial of legitimacy and "generalizations [that] assert by condemning their opposite the values of the society where the assertion is being made." [14]

We can see, perhaps, in the apocryphal Acts a social situation wherein charismatic leaders of infant Christian communities were accused of sorcery by members of Greco-Roman society because of their asocial teachings and because of their undefined place in the larger social order, *not* because their charismatic activities fell afoul of laws against magic. Indeed, were such activities often considered illegal, Christian apologists would have been less than willing to brag of them as proofs of Christian doctrine.

To convert to those Christian teachings, then, was dangerous; those converted would be in danger from sorcery or witchcraft accusations insofar as they adopted and shared the asocial ideals promulgated in the apocryphal Acts. The accusations seem to have originated from the masses, from people in general, rather than from judicial authorities.

Those who composed the apocryphal Acts would have shown themselves in a more positive light had they simply claimed that accusations that Christians did illegal magic were completely false; they could have argued that the apostles spoke no incantations and only healed for moral purposes. If they did defend the faith in that fashion, they did not do so in the context of sorcery accusations. Rather, they mirrored in the Acts a real situation, a dangerous situation, one where accusations were grounded in the undeniable facts of their asocial, or socially interstitial, principles and form of life. The community behind the apocryphal Acts seems to have been one of persons who had chosen to go outside the normal structure of their own society, who perhaps were faced with sorcery or witchcraft accusations themselves and who heartened themselves with tales of glorious apostles similarly accused.

To this point we have been considering matters which show the relationship between apostles and the social environment in which they lived. It is time to turn to the relationship between apostles and their adherents, to examine the intra-community realities re-

14. Mair, *Witchcraft*, p. 203.

flected in the apocryphal Acts. We will first look at the event of conversion and see that in the Acts conversion is often brought about by charismatic activity, "proofs" both of the charismatic leadership of the apostles and of their preaching. The charismatic leader is an ambiguous figure, preaching Christianity but often being treated as if he were divine in his own right. As we shall see, exalting the apostle tended to increase the community's emotional dependence upon an undependable (i.e., itinerant) leader.

While the apostle is one who brings the Christian message to people, he does not often convince people of the truth of that message by sheer argument. His message is usually validated by means of charismatic actions. Throughout the apocryphal Acts there are numerous examples of conversions which occur because of immediate existential evidence.

In the Acts of John, after a group of aged women are brought to the theater, the apostle says:

I have been sent, then, on no human mission, nor on a useless journey; nor am I a merchant that makes bargains or exchanges; but Jesus Christ, whom I preach, in his mercy and goodness is converting you all, you who are held fast in unbelief and enslaved by shameful desires; and through me he wills to deliver you from your error; and by his power I will convict even your praetor's disbelief, by raising up these women who are lying before you— you see what a state and what sicknesses they are in. And I cannot do this if they perish; and so they shall all be helped by healing (A.Jn. 33).

John's healings were apparently not entirely convincing, for he complains: "How many miracles (and) cures of diseases have you seen (performed) through me? And yet you are blinded in your hearts, and cannot recover your sight" (A.Jn. 39). The apostle then destroys the local temple, killing the priest. "And the people rising from the ground went running and threw down the rest of the idol temple, crying out, 'The God of John (is the) only (God) we know; from now on we worship him, since he has had mercy upon us!' And as John came down from that place a great crowd took hold of him, saying, 'Help us, John; stand by us, for we perish in vain. You see our purpose; you see the people following after you, hanging in hope upon your God'" (A.Jn. 44). Works and not words are the fundamental strength supporting John's missionary endeavors.

Some Christians in the Acts of Peter attribute their faith to miracles, saying "We believe in him whom Paul preached to us; for through him we have seen the dead raised up and (men) delivered from various infirmities" (A.Pt. 2:4). Marcellus, who has returned to the faith after falling under the sway of Simon Magus, undertakes to repair a fragmented statue and says, "I am being tested by thine apostle Peter whether I truly believe in thy holy name" (A.Pt. 4:11). When he takes water in his hands and sprinkles the water on the statue, it is miraculously repaired. Marcellus then exults because, "this first miracle was done by his hands; and he therefore believed with his whole heart in the name of Jesus Christ the Son of God, through whom all things impossible are (made) possible" (A.Pt. 4:11). Again in the Acts of Peter, the apostle convinces people of his teachings when he takes a dried fish and says to the people, "If you now see this swimming in the water like a fish, will you be able to believe in him whom I preach?" And the people respond, "Indeed we will believe you!" (A.Pt. 5:13). Peter himself says, "We must put no faith in words but in actions and deeds" (A.Pt. 6:17).

Evidence for this manner of conversion is present in each of the apocryphal Acts. In a surviving précis of the Acts of Andrew (A.An. 4, James), a proconsul and his whole house are baptized after Andrew calls up an earthquake and, so to speak, puts the fear of God into them. The apostle raises an Egyptian boy beloved of Demetrius of Amasea and "all believed and were baptized" (A.An. 3, James). In the Acts of Paul the people cry out, "One is God who has made heaven and earth, who has given life to the daughter (. . .) of Paul" (A.Pl. 8) after that apostle raises a girl from the dead. The Acts of Thomas reports: "The fame of him spread into all the towns and villages, and all who had sick or such as were troubled by unclean spirits brought them, and laid them on the road by which he was to pass, and he healed them all in the power of the Lord. Then all who were healed by him said with one accord with one voice: 'Glory be to thee, Jesus, who (to all) alike hast granted healing through thy servant and apostle Thomas! And being in health and rejoicing we beseech thee that we may become (members) of thy flock and be numbered among thy sheep'" (A.Th. 6:59). Here again charismatic efficacy leads to belief.

We can conclude from such reports that, if the apocryphal Acts reflect anything of a social situation, they reflect a community where the power of charismatic action was proof positive of religious doctrine, a community largely composed of people who took for granted the fact that special Christians could heal the sick and raise the dead in order to bring new adherents into the faith. We saw earlier that even for the most intellectual Christians charismatic efficacy was an important apologetic device. Since charismatic effects bring about conversion throughout the apocryphal Acts, it is possible that many of those who compiled and heard the Acts were themselves made Christian by such means.

The charismatic apostle in the Acts is an ambivalent figure, supposed to be human but often treated as divine. This difficulty is never fully resolved. In the Acts of Peter the apostle clearly spells out his mortal nature: "You men of Rome, seeing that I too am one of you, wearing human flesh, and a sinner, but have obtained mercy, do not look at me, as though by my own power I were doing what I do; (the power is) my Lord Jesus Christ's, who is the judge of the living and of the dead. Believing in him and sent by him, I dare to entreat him to raise the dead" (A.Pt. 8:28). Thomas gives a similar discourse toward the end of his Acts. "I am not Jesus, but a servant of Jesus. I am not Christ, but I am a minister of Christ. I am not the Son of god, but I pray to be counted worthy with him" (A.Th. Mart. 160). In both cases the apostle's human nature is made clear to an audience for which such clarifications were necessary, just as Peter and Paul are reported in the canonical Acts of the Apostles to have found it necessary to make such disclaimers.

We can see the necessity of such clarifications. In the Acts of Peter the apostle raises a child from the dead. "From that same hour they venerated him as a god" (A.Pt. 8:29). Never is this action disapproved. The Acts of Thomas reports that "the crowd worshipped him as a god" (A.Th. 9:106). Here we have evidence that in the community behind the apocryphal Acts charismatic leaders were thought of ambivalently. Certainly their Christian message and their own protestations indicate that Thomas and Peter are only human, yet they are still occasionally worshipped.

In the Acts of John Stateus, who has just been raised, "arose and worshipped the apostle" (A.Jn. 17, James). In another passage the newly converted priest of all the idols "worshipped John" and ran to the proconsul to say to him, "he is a god hidden in the form of a man" (A.Jn. 21, James). John even goes so far as to identify himself with God in the process of uttering an incantation to raise up a dead woman. The apostle goes to her and says: "He speaks, whom every ruler fears, and every creature, power, abyss and all darkness and unsmiling death, the heights of heaven and the circles of hell, the resurrection of the dead and the sight of the blind, the whole power of the prince of this world and the pride of its ruler. Arise (he says) and be not an excuse for many who wish to disbelieve" (A.Jn. 23). This sort of self-identification with deity is a common technique in Hellenistic magic. Peter Brown says that it is "what the psycho-analyst would call 'introjective identification,' that is, he becomes the god—'for Thou art I and I am Thou: whatever I say must come to pass.'"[15] There is no evidence that the apostles deliberately intended themselves to be taken for gods, but the use of such a technique would certainly lead to confusion in that regard. Apostles do seem to have been occasionally regarded as divine, and to have voiced opposition to that notion.

We cannot find in the Acts a clear conception of the apostle as fully divine, as a divine man, or as an entirely human person. Rather, what we encounter is a situation of flux, of ambiguity, of tension between a Christian message emphasizing the humanity of all Christians and the facts of Christian life where divine power acting through charismatic individuals was a common cause of conversion and adherence to the faith. Even resurrection appearances were no special prerogative of Jesus for, remarkably enough, Peter (A.Pt. 9:40), Paul (A.Pl. 11:6–7), and Thomas (A.Th. 13:170) all appear to their followers after death. From all this we can catch a glimpse of a community, one which was in part made Christian through the acts of charismatic leaders, but which was unable to give up entirely the notion that those leaders themselves ought to be worshipped.

The community of Christians responsible for the Acts appears to have been emotionally dependent upon revered apostles. Those apostles, however, do not remain with their followers; they are itinerant, traveling at the urging of visions. John is brought to Lycomedes by a vision (A.Jn. 18). In the Acts of Andrew it is said that, "Many asked him to lodge with them, but he said he could

15. Brown, *Religion and Society*, pp. 139–40.

only go where God bade him" (A.An. 22). One group of Christians, bereft at the idea of Paul's leaving, had their grief brought upon them because Paul, having fasted for three days, "saw a vision, the Lord saying to him, 'Paul, arise and be a physician to those who are in Spain'" (A.Pt. 1:1). Charismatic leaders in the Acts are led from town to town by visions; their itinerancy is both required and inspired.

Once conversions are effected by the apostles, those converted seem often to have viewed the physical presence of the apostles as a principal means by which they might remain Christian. Apostles, however, are itinerant by definition; and in the apocryphal Acts all apostles stay on the move until their deaths.

Evidence that the itinerancy of the apostle was considered to be a difficulty by the community is present in all the Acts. In the Acts of Peter Paul is determined to leave Rome, but,

great lamentation arose among all the brotherhood because they believed that they would not see Paul again, so that they even rent their clothes. Besides, they had in view that Paul had often contended with the Jewish teachers and had confuted them (saying), "It is Christ on whom your fathers laid hands. He abolished their sabbath and fasts and festivals and circumcision and he abolished the doctrines of men and the other traditions." But the brethren besought Paul by the coming of our Lord Jesus Christ that he should not stay away longer than a year; and they said, "We know your love for your brethren; do not forget us when you arrive there (in Spain), or begin to desert us like little children without their mother." (A.Pt. 1:1)

The brethren continued weeping and entreated the Lord with Paul and said, "Lord Jesus Christ, be thou with Paul, and restore him to us unharmed; for we know our weakness which is still with us" (A.Pt. 1:1–2).

We can see here that the Acts not only suppose that the departure of the apostle is difficult for the people to accept, but also that the people may even thereafter fall away from Christianity. In this particular case they turn to the next itinerant wonder-worker to come to town, Simon Magus. When Peter faces execution, the Christians of Rome plead with him to avoid death: "They were grieved at heart, and said with tears, 'We entreat you, Peter, take thought for us that are young'" (A.Pt. 9:36).

In the Acts of Andrew a converted Christian expresses his horror at learning that Andrew will soon be martyred. He cannot conceive of remaining faithful in Andrew's absence and says:

That part of my soul which inclines to the things I hear is being punished because it has a presentiment of the distress that comes after this. For you yourself go away and I know well that you will do it nobly. Where and in whom shall I seek and find hereafter your care and love? When you were the sower I received the seeds of the words of salvation. And for these to sprout and grow up there is need of no other than yourself, most blessed Andrew. And what else have I to say to you than this? I need the great mercy and help that comes from you, to be able to be worthy of the seed I have from you, which will only grow permanently and emerge into the light if you wish it and pray for it and for my whole self (A.An. Cod. Vat. 12).

His outcry is significant for, again, we can see the fear of people converted by a charismatic leader that in the absence of that person their faith will be in jeopardy.

In the Acts of John Lycomedes says to that apostle, "I beg and entreat you in God's name through whom you raised us up, to stay with us, both you and your companions. . . . There is no hope for us in your God, but we shall have been raised in vain, if you do not stay with us" (A.Jn. 25). Again we hear the voice of one converted by a miracle faced with loss of faith if the one who produced the miracle departs. Another example occurs in the Acts of Paul when the brethren, after Paul has announced his imminent departure, "lifted up their voice and said: 'O God, (. . .) Father of Christ, help thou Paul thy servant, that he may yet abide with us because of our weakness'" (A.Pl. 9).

Finally, there is a report in the Acts of Thomas of a woman exorcised of a demon. The demon says to her,

Abide in peace, since thou hast taken refuge in one greater than I; but I will depart and seek one like thee, and if I find her not I return to thee again. For I know that while thou art near to this man thou hast thy refuge with him, but when he is gone thou shalt be as thou wert before he appeared, and him shalt thou forget, but for me there shall be opportunity and confidence; but now I fear the name of him who hath saved thee (A.Th. 5:46).

The woman, however, receives baptism, which seems to render her immune to demonic threats.

These observations allow us to conclude that the community behind the apocryphal Acts was somewhat tenuous. Individuals were sometimes converted by means of charismatic actions and were then devoted nearly as much to the apostle himself as to the God he proclaimed. When his mission and his visions caused the apostle to depart, the Christians devoted to him faced emotional devastation and feared that their faith might weaken. Nevertheless, many evidently remained Christian, performed Christian ritual in communal fashion, and composed apocryphal Acts.

Gerd Theissen's *Sociology of Early Palestinian Christianity* is a brilliant work which only came to our attention after this study was almost completed. In this book he makes a persuasive case that teaching authority and community authority in the earliest Christian church was in the hands of wandering charismatics. These persons are strikingly similar to the apostles this study discovers in the apocryphal Acts. Indeed, if Theissen's results can be taken seriously, and there is good reason to believe that this book will be a seminal work for the next decade of scholarship, then the immediate followers of Jesus, and probably therefore Jesus himself, were persons much more like the apostles reflected in the apocryphal Acts than like the staid, educated, and philosophically sophisticated persons who are known as the fathers of the church. If Theissen is correct, the sociological heirs of Jesus are the wandering charismatic apostles of the second century, the persons who inspired the apocryphal Acts.

We are faced with the problem of understanding the kind of Christian person who shared in the apostles' asocial virtues, who was emotionally dependent upon undependable itinerant bearers of charisma, and yet who must have had some sort of relationship to a church structure stable enough to permit the composition and promulgation of the apocryphal Acts themselves. The foregoing parts of this study describe the world of the original community behind the Acts and the difficulties its members encountered. The following parts of this study attempt to describe some of the major characteristics of the people who formed that community.

IV

Women in the Apocryphal Acts

THE DOCUMENTS now known as apocryphal Acts were written by Christians in the Roman Empire in the period from approximately 160 to 225 A.D. They were written from within a particular community of Christians—a community somewhat outside the normal boundaries of society in the ancient world, a community which placed an exceptionally high value on sexual continence. It will be our contention that the Acts derive from communities of continent Christian women, the widows of their church, who were both adherents of apostles and participants in a stable church structure. This hypothesis, which may seem rather startling, will be shown in the following pages to be both highly probable and in accord with the values inherent in the Acts.

The Acts are not documents intended for the use of missionaries to pagan people; they were written for an audience already converted, an audience which would enjoy tales of glorious Christian apostles and of pagans joining the faith in great numbers. They may, furthermore, have been partly intended for missionary use within the Christian community—perhaps written by Christians who valued sexual continence for other Christians who did not.

In the second century, it must be remembered, monasticism did not yet exist and neither did the requirement of celibacy for clergy. Yet the original community behind the Acts valued sexual continence above almost everything else. Knowing this, we may presume that this community was made up of Christians of a particular sort—Christians who lived sexually continent lives.

The strong emphasis in the Acts on a sexually continent life-style means that those who compiled the Acts were acutely aware of human gender. In other words, the sexes and attitudes toward sexuality of the characters featured in the Acts are not products of chance. Of course, in some religious tales the sexes of the characters may be of no real consequence. However, in religious tales focused overwhelmingly on the issue of sexual continence and the accompanying problem of the relationships between men and women, the gender of the characters is obviously an essential component. Indications that one sex or the other is valued more highly, or is the subject of greater concern, are significant. Such indications are particularly important when they appear as repeated themes in a series of similar stories. In an effort to determine the composition of the original community behind the Acts, we can consider the relationships between the sexes as they are depicted in the Acts. In addition, we must try to reveal the prevailing attitudes toward men and women expressed in the Acts by describing the traits of those principal characters who appear to be most highly valued.

Our search for the original community behind the Acts is a search for a Christian community of a particular and rather unusual kind. We seek a community for whom sexual continence was a primary value and a way of life, one for whom the distinctions of gender were vitally important. Our question becomes this: Was the Acts' original community made up predominantly of continent male Christians, continent female Christians, or of continent Christians of both sexes in roughly equal numbers?

"The apocryphal Acts are designed for entertainment, instruction and edification," wrote Wilhelm Schneemelcher, and he is entirely correct.[1] This simple statement gives us a clue to the sexually continent community behind the Acts. One of the fundamental ways edification proceeds in any religious document is the relating of faith to circumstances, showing what it would be like to live in accordance with the principles of the faith. When edification is attempted through fiction or storytelling, faith is related to circum-

---

1. Schneemelcher and Hennecke, eds., *New Testament Apocrypha*, p. 273.

stances by the creation of figures who embody the ideal of the faith. These ideal figures serve as role models for members of the community.

To begin to learn about this community, we can try to determine what sort of person would have been edified by the Acts. To do this, we should first determine what kind of role models or exemplary persons are established in the Acts. The type of person most prominently held up for approbation in the Acts would have served as a role model for both the type of Christian person who predominated in the original community of the Acts and for those persons encouraged to adopt the life-style of that community.

The apostles themselves could not have been role models for members of a community; by their itinerancy they are external to any permanent community. Defined by their charisma they are leaders, not followers. A community might receive and appreciate apostles, but it could not be composed of apostles. Nor could it be that the Acts were the products of second-century apostles creating role models for themselves. Apostles, possessors of personal charisma, had their model in Christ, the source of their power. The fabulous exploits and exaggerated deeds of John, Paul, Thomas, Peter, and Andrew could not be accomplished by ordinary humans. A charismatic leader, dependent on his powers to "prove" his leadership and his doctrine, risked undermining his own claims to authority by unfavorably contrasting himself with the mightier men of the century past. The community behind the Acts is most probably reflected in the audiences of apostles described in the Acts. Exemplary figures in those audiences might have served as role models for members of the continent Christian community from which the Acts came. Very often these figures are women.

The apocryphal Acts often present the martyrdom of the apostle as the climax of his exemplary piety. At this conclusion of his mission, he leaves behind evidence of his successful efforts, perfect converts and exemplars. In the Acts of Andrew and the Acts of Thomas, the concluding, climactic martyrdom sequences contain tales and descriptions of ideal Christian women. After discussing them, we will turn our attention to the Acts of John and of Peter.

As the final sequence of the Acts of Andrew begins, a Christian woman named Iphidamia leads the apostle to the sickbed of another woman, Maximilla, wife of the local proconsul (A.An. 30, James).

Maximilla, after being cured by the apostle Andrew, is portrayed as a model of Christian perfection. Determined to remain continent, she removes herself from her husband. Her chastity and faith survive all attacks. The apostle addresses a lengthy discourse to her, seeing in her the epitome of the Christian person. "I know that you are more powerful than those who seem to overpower you, more glorious than those who are casting you down in shame, than those who are leading you away to imprisonment. If, O man [*sic*], you understand all these things in yourself, namely that you are immaterial, holy, light, akin to the unbegotten, intellectual, heavenly, translucent, pure, superior to the flesh, superior to the world, superior to powers, superior to authorities over whom you really are, . . . then take knowledge in what you are superior" (A.An. Cod. Vat. 6). Led by the Lord in Andrew's likeness, Maximilla and Iphidamia come to the prison to hear Andrew. These two alone are privileged to see the Lord. They are models for the ideal Christian: continent, resolute, and akin to him that is unbegotten.

Except for the apostle, only two other figures are of importance in this climactic martyrdom sequence: the wicked proconsul (deserted by Maximilla) and his brother, Stratocles. The latter is converted to Christianity; but, because he fails to appreciate that Andrew's impending death is for the best, he is repeatedly upbraided by the apostle. Andrew, on one occasion, turns from an address directed to Maximilla to speak to Stratocles. "'But you, Stratocles,' he said, looking at him, 'why are you so distressed with many tears and why do you sigh so audibly? Why your despondency? Why your great pain and great grief? You know what has been said, and why then do I beseech you as (my) child to be in control of yourself?'" (A.An. Cod. Vat. 10) At another time Stratocles loses his temper with those who torment Andrew. The apostle scolds him, saying: "My child Stratocles, I wish that for the future you would possess your soul unmoved and would reject such a thing [as anger] so that you neither inwardly respond to the wicked intentions (of men) nor outwardly be inflamed" (A.An. Mart. 2.3). Stratocles, at another point, misapprehends the apostle's crucifixion. "And Stratocles asked him: 'Why do you smile, slave of God? Your laughter makes us mourn and weep because we are being deprived of you.' And the blessed Andrew answered him: 'Shall I not laugh, my child Stratocles, at the vain plot of Aegeates by which he intends to avenge himself on us?'" (A.An. Mart. 2.5) Stratocles is depicted as one who only partially understands Andrew's teachings. Maximilla, on the other hand, is effusively praised. In fact, she seems to assist in Andrew's salvation. "As Adam died in Eve because of the harmony of their relationship, so even now I live in you who keep the command of the Lord and who give yourself over to the state (dignity) of your (true) being" (A.An. Cod. Vat. 7).

The woman Maximilla can be taken to be an ideal role model for Christians who would be continent, resolute, and perfect. Greater praise is accorded her than the man Stratocles.

Only one other segment of the Acts of Andrew survives in anything like its original form. In this fragment we hear of a young soldier, possessed by a demon who says, "Truly, O man of god, I have never destroyed a limb of his because of the holy hands of his sister" (A.An. Utrecht 14:32–35). The soldier is protected by "a sister, a virgin, who is a great ascetic and champion. Truly, I say, she is near to God because of her purity and her prayers and her alms" (A.An. Utrecht 13:6–11). Apparently the story also described that woman's defeat of a demon attack conjured up by a magician as well as a vision of Christ the woman had during which Christ told her that Andrew would heal her brother. In this fragmentary segment, as in the martyrdom sequence of the Acts of Andrew, a continent Christian woman is highly honored, held up for imitation, and is shown to be somewhat superior in piety to a man.

Something quite similar takes place at the conclusion of the Acts of Thomas (A.Th. 9–13). There a woman, Mygdonia, is converted to a life of Christian continence and is portrayed as an ideal Christian. Not only does she renounce her husband, but she also adopts a life of poverty. Furthermore, she successfully converts both Tertia, the wife of the king, and Marcia, her nurse, to Christianity, endures imprisonment, and anoints the women she converted after the apostle has baptized them.

Except for Thomas himself and for the villainous husbands of Mygdonia and Tertia, only two males appear in the last half of the Acts of Thomas. One is Siphor, a character in a long story focused on his wife and daughter (A.Th. 7–8); the other is Vazan the son of the king. Vazan's conversion follows that of Mygdonia, Marcia and Tertia (A.Th. 12). Both men play secondary roles in the narrative.

Mygdonia is not contrasted favorably with them (as is Maximilla with Stratocles) but with the apostle himself. Mygdonia's husband, Charisius, threatens Thomas with death if he will not encourage Mygdonia to return to him. The apostle then says: "'My daughter Mygdonia, obey what brother Charisius says!' And Mygdonia said: 'If thou couldst not (name) the deed in word, (how) dost thou compel me to endure the act? . . . But now (thou sayest this) because thou art afraid. But who that has done something and been praised for the work changes it? . . . Who finding a treasure did not make use of it?'" (A.Th. 10:130) Mygdonia shows herself capable of holding fast to continence even in the face of cowardly apostolic advice to the contrary.

Both Thomas and Stratocles are unfavorably contrasted with women converts. We shall see that this sort of contrast can be found in the other Acts. The featured women Maximilla and Mygdonia were exemplary models for members of the community behind the Acts, figures featured at the Acts' climactic moments.

An exemplary person is present in the Acts of John not at the occasion of the death of the apostle (which in these Acts is an anticlimactic natural death) but in the middle of these Acts in a lengthy sequence only partially preserved. This person is the woman Drusiana who, having been converted to the faith, determines to live continently. Her husband, Andronicus, locks her in a tomb but she weathers that ordeal and, while in the tomb, sees a vision of Christ as a youth and as John (A.Jn. 87). The impressive Round Dance visionary sequence of the Acts of John (A.Jn. 88–103) is an extended elucidation of Drusiana's vision of the Lord. Drusiana eventually convinces her husband to join her in a life of Christian continence (A.Jn. 63).

Drusiana's understanding of the faith is favorably contrasted with that of a Christian man, Callimachus. He tells John not to raise the villainous Fortunatus, but the apostle remonstrates with him, telling him, "My son, we have not learned to return evil for evil. . . . If then you will not have me raise up Fortunatus, it is a task for Drusiana" (A.Jn. 81). The woman raises him successfully. Drusiana, continent, enduring, and capable of performing the charismatic action of raising the dead, could easily be an exemplary model of piety for a community of continent Christian women dwelling in a world where such actions are taken to be crucial to the

propagation of Christianity. While Drusiana's husband, Andronicus, and Callimachus are both important to the story, they become
acceptable characters only after Drusiana has weathered their as-
saults. She, and not those men, is the exemplary figure.

The Acts of John also tells of a couple named Lycomedes and
Cleopatra. The fundamental contrast of this story is on the different
powers of self-control possessed by the man and the woman. Cleopatra lies dying. Her husband has very little faith in the power of
John to heal her, even though the arrival of John was announced to
him by a vision of God. He laments her loss in a lengthy passage
(A.Jn. 20). Finally,

And Lycomedes still speaking to Cleopatra approached her bed and lamented with a loud voice.

But John pulled him away and said, "Cease from these lamentations and
from these unfitting words of yours. It is not proper for you who saw the
vision to be unbelieving for you shall receive your consort again. . . . Call
on the Lord, entreat him for your consort and he shall revive her." But he
fell upon the ground and lamented with all his soul.

John therefore said with tears, "Alas for the fresh betrayal of my vision!"
(A.Jn. 21)

John subsequently raises Cleopatra from the dead. She learns that
her husband has died of grief and reacts in a fashion markedly in
contrast to the excessive lamentations of Lycomedes:

And when Cleopatra came with John into her bedroom and saw Lycomedes dead on her account she lost her voice, and ground her teeth and bit her
tongue, and closed her eyes, raining down tears; and she quietly attended to
the apostle.

But John had pity upon Cleopatra when he saw her neither raging nor
distraught, and called upon the perfect and condescending mercy, and said,
"Lord Jesus Christ, thou seest (her) distress, thou seest (her) need, thou
seest Cleopatra crying out her soul in silence; for she contains within her
the intolerable raging (of her sorrow)" (A.Jn. 24).

John then turns to Cleopatra (A.Jn. 24) and advises her to say to her
husband, "Rise up and glorify the name of God, since to the dead
he gives (back) the dead." She does so and Lycomedes is raised.

Cleopatra is a model of self-control, Lycomedes a model of excessive emotion. Cleopatra has faith enough to raise her husband; Lycomedes does not even attempt to raise his wife. The exemplary model is the woman, not the man.

In the next sequence of the Acts of John, Lycomedes has a portrait painted of the apostle. John is offended by this gesture and complains to Lycomedes, "What you have now done is childish and imperfect; you have drawn a dead likeness of what is dead" (A.Jn. 29). As Drusiana was favorably compared with Callimachus, so Cleopatra is favorably contrasted with Lycomedes. Even after having been raised from the dead by his wife, Lycomedes shows such an imperfect understanding of the faith that John must reprove him.

The Acts of Peter does not focus on any single exemplary figure. However, the martyrdom sequence of Peter's Acts is valuable for our purpose of showing that continent Christian women formed the greater part of the original community behind the apocryphal Acts. That sequence begins with the conversion of Agrippina, Nicaria, Euphemia, and Doris who are concubines of the prefect Agrippa (A.Pt. 9:33). They are joined by

one woman who was especially beautiful, the wife of Albinus the friend of Caesar, Xanthippe by name, [who] came with the other ladies to Peter, and she too separated from Albinus. He therefore, filled with fury and passionate love for Xanthippe, and amazed that she would not even sleep in the same bed with him, was raging like a wild beast and wished to do away with Peter; for he knew that he was responsible for her leaving his bed. And many other women besides fell in love with the doctrine of purity and separated from their husbands, and men too ceased to sleep with their own wives, since they wished to worship God in sobriety and purity (A.Pt. 9:34).

The tale would have us envision the martyrdom of the apostle occurring in the context of a crowd of pious women; that men too become Christian is but an afterthought of the author of the Acts of Peter.

The remainder of the martyrdom sequence mentions only two characters by name: Xanthippe, who warns Peter of her husband's plot against him, and the Christian man Marcellus. A man of much wealth, Marcellus was once an adherent of Simon Magus but he has returned to the faith; his story is a parallel to the story, told earlier in the Acts of Peter, of Eubula, a wealthy woman who turned away from Simon Magus to the apostle (A.Pt. 6:17). At the conclusion of the Acts of Peter the resurrected apostle appears to Marcellus and scolds him for spending money on burial expenses: "The things which you laid out for the dead, you have lost; for you who are alive were like a dead man caring for the dead" (A.Pt. 9:40). He is imperfect in his faith just as was Lycomedes in the Acts of John.

Maximilla, Mygdonia, Drusiana, and Cleopatra are all exemplary in their piety, their continence, their endurance of tribulation. All can be seen to have been possible role models for pious and continent Christian women; all are shown to be somewhat superior to certain Christian men during the course of the narratives focused on them. Except for the apostles themselves, in the Acts of Andrew, Thomas, John, and Peter no male Christians are as favored, or as highly praised, as the women discussed above. The Acts of Paul, as we shall see, shows Thecla to be an exemplary female Christian but, far from being unique, the focus on Thecla's virtue in Paul's Acts is matched by a focus on the virtue of pious women in other Acts.

In the Acts of Paul Thecla of Iconium is presented as a model of continence, resolute against the urgings of her betrothed and her mother, capable of fighting off the advances of a rich man who falls in love with her (A.Pl. 3:1–43). She endures imprisonment and torture without flinching. She is devoted to Paul and to Christ without reservation and baptizes herself after Paul has refused to do so. At the conclusion of the story focused on her we find her back in her home community prepared to preach the Gospel. Like Mygdonia, Maximilla, Cleopatra, and Drusiana, Thecla is an exceptional Christian and a model for a continent Christian life. Also like those women, Thecla is favorably contrasted with a Christian man, the apostle Paul himself.

Thecla's first round of tortures in the arena qualifies her as a confessor of the faith. Paul, however, deserts her in her time of trial. The Acts tells it this way: "But Thecla sought for Paul, as a lamb in the wilderness looks about for the shepherd. And when she looked upon the crowd, she saw the Lord sitting in the form of Paul and said: 'As if I were not able to endure, Paul has come to look after me.' And she looked steadily at him; but he departed into the heavens" (A.Pl. 3:21). Paul and even Christ in the form of Paul desert Thecla when she looks for their support. Through the intervention of God she survives and seeks after Paul. He has been fasting in her behalf but decides to end the fast without having heard of her rescue (A.Pl. 3:22). Although the apostle certainly supports her cause, the fact that he determines to end his fast without knowing of her rescue indicates that his support is weak.

Thecla, now a confessor, comes to Paul and tells him that she will cut her hair and follow him. Paul does not believe her, seeing her not as a Christian and a confessor but as a beautiful female. "And Thecla said to Paul: 'I will cut my hair short and follow thee wherever thou goest.' But he said: 'The season is unfavourable, and thou art comely. May no other temptation come upon thee worse than the first, and thou endure not and play the coward!'" (A.Pl. 3:25) Paul sees Thecla's beauty, not her piety. He does not trust her, although she trusts him; and he does not baptize her. Her trust in Paul is shown to have been misplaced, for soon after,

a Syrian by the name of Alexander, one of the first of the Antiochenes, seeing Thecla fell in love with her, and sought to win over Paul with money and gifts. But Paul said: "I do not know the woman of whom thou dost speak, nor is she mine." But he, being a powerful man, embraced her on the open street; she however would not endure it, but looked about for Paul and cried out bitterly, saying: "Force not the stranger, force not the handmaid of God! Among the Iconians I am one of the first, and because I did not wish to marry Thamyris I have been cast out of the city." And taking hold of Alexander she ripped his cloak, took off the crown from his head, and made him a laughing-stock (A.Pl. 3:26).

Paul does not respond to her calls for help and, apparently, vanishes from the scene. As she did in the arena, when Paul and Jesus in the form of Paul had deserted her, Thecla struggles alone and successfully.

Alexander has her condemned to the beasts in the arena for a second round of tortures. Nothing is heard of the apostle. She survives the tortures and baptizes herself. Again Thecla seeks Paul. Finding him, she discovers that he still fails to appreciate her piety even though, to indicate that she is not to be regarded only as a beautiful woman, she "sewed her mantle into a cloak after the fashion of men" (A.Pl. 3:40). Paul "was astonished when he saw her and the crowd that was with her, pondering whether another temptation was not upon her" (A.Pl. 3:40). Her repeated endurance has not convinced him, her symbolic garb does not convince him. He still apprehends her as a woman subject to temptation.

Thecla's struggle is threefold: First, she must avoid the advances of her betrothed husband and the Syrian Alexander, who desire her as a female. Second, she must endure the torments of civil authorities, who punish her because of her determined sexual continence. Third, she must struggle to break through Paul's misapprehension of her as nothing more than a beautiful woman, weak and subject to temptation. Thecla's exemplary piety can be taken to be a model for that of pious women. Her struggles against the advances of lustful men and the disrespect of pious men may well be a reflection of the kind of difficulties pious Christian women encountered from men in their communities.

The author of the Acts of Paul abstracts Thecla's struggle with men into a general opposition of males to females. We can see this theme repeated again and again in the story of Thecla's second round of tortures. According to this story, Thecla is befriended by a queen, but opposed by Alexander and the local governor. After the governor's condemnation of her, "the women were panic-stricken, and cried out before the judgment-seat: 'An evil judgment! A godless judgment!'" (A.Pl. 3:27). Nevertheless, Thecla is bound to a female lion who does her no harm but licks her feet.

Alexander comes to take Thecla away, but the queen drives him off. Thecla then intervenes with God on behalf of the queen's daughter who died outside the faith. Thecla finally is taken to the arena. Then, "there was a tumult, and roaring of the beasts, and a shouting of the people and of the women who sat together, some saying: 'Bring in the sacrilegious one!' but the women saying: 'May the city perish for this lawlessness! Slay us all, Proconsul! A bitter sight, an evil judgment!'" (A.Pl. 3:32)

Thecla is attacked by a lion, but a lioness rescues her and both beasts die. "And lions and bears were set upon her, and a fierce lioness ran to her and lay down at her feet. And the crowd of the women raised a great shout. And a bear ran upon her, but the lioness ran and met it, and tore the bear asunder. And again a lion trained against men, which belonged to Alexander, ran upon her; and the lioness grappled with the lion, and perished with it. And the women mourned the more, since the lioness which helped her was dead" (A.Pl. 3:33). More beasts are put into the arena to attack Thecla, but "the women cried aloud, and some threw petals, others nard, others cassia, others amomum, so that there was an abundance of perfumes. And all the beasts let loose were overpowered as if by sleep, and did not touch her" (A.Pl. 3:35).

Thecla's torments finally end when the queen faints and appears dead. The governor, taken in by this ruse, fears that Caesar will be angry at the death of his kinswoman and decides to cease the attempt to execute Thecla. She preaches a short sermon to the governor who is, apparently, converted. He says to the queen, "I release to you Thecla the pious handmaid of God," and immediately thereafter, "all the women cried out with a loud voice, and as with one mouth gave praise to God, saying: 'One is God, who has delivered Thecla!', so that all the city was shaken by the sound" (A.Pl. 3:38). The story concludes with Thecla's conversion of the queen's maidservants.

A theme we have discussed earlier in reference to other Acts reaches a peak in this tale: the piety of women is favorably contrasted with that of men. A queen supports Thecla; male rulers oppose her. Maidservants are converted; menservants are not mentioned. Women repeatedly support Thecla and even act to subdue the beasts; the other people cry out for her execution. Even a lioness supports her against the attack of other beasts.

Those Christians who composed and heard the Acts of Paul would have been entirely in support of Thecla during her struggle in the arena. They would have been rooting for the brave confessor of the faith as the story was told. The audience *in* the story and the audience *of* the story may perhaps be identified with each other. Women who might have found in Thecla a model for their own continent Christian lives would have identified themselves with the women in the story who demanded that her execution be stopped. The whole Thecla sequence in the Acts of Paul would have had considerable appeal to an audience of continent Christian women who in their own lives had discovered that Christian men still apprehended them in sexual terms and, therefore, did not take them seriously.

The exemplary piety of women is recounted in other sections of the Acts of Paul, sections that are only preserved in fragments. The daughter of a Christian couple lies dead; both parents lament but the mother of the girl seems to have asked Paul to raise her (A.Pl. 8). This theme is repeated in another fragment when the son of a Christian couple lies dead. Both parents mourn, and the father "mourned for he loved Dion more than his other son. [Yet] he sat at Paul's feet and forgot that Dion was dead" (A.Pl. 3, James). The mother, however, requests that Dion be raised and he is. We cannot say much about such fragmentary episodes, but it seems to be the case in both instances that the mother has greater faith in the apostle's capabilities than does her husband.

Another fragmentary episode reports that a spirit (of prophecy) comes on a man. He announces that Paul must depart. The community is bereft at this news, but a spirit comes upon a woman named Myrta who remonstrates with them. "Brethren, why (are you alarmed at the sight of this sign?) Paul the servant of the Lord will save many in Rome, and will nourish many with the word, so that there is no number (to count them)" (A.Pl. 9). The community becomes at ease again. Here the spiritual announcement of a woman resolves a difficulty brought on the community by the spirit speaking through a man. At another place in Paul's Acts two women hold an agape attended by the apostle (A.Pl. Appendix). Thus, we see that the attitude toward women evidenced in the well-preserved Thecla sequence is not by any means unique to that section of the Acts of Paul.

The martyrdom sequence of the Acts of Paul (A.Pl. 11:1–7) contains no mention of women, a fact which, in light of their importance in all other martyrdom sequences in the Acts, is rather surprising. Quite a number of men are therein converted from being soldiers of Nero to being soldiers of Christ. None is singled out for special attention or made into a model for emulation. Perhaps the author of the Acts of Paul, having so powerfully stressed the virtues of women in the Thecla sequence, felt compelled to write a conclusion stressing the potential for Christian piety among men. On the other hand, perhaps that author, so sensitive to the problems of Christian women, did not wish to portray the apostle as having been executed because of his conversions of women for fear of undermining the notion that the conversion of women is a good thing.

The figures of Drusiana, Cleopatra, Maximilla, Mygdonia, and Thecla are all impressive models of piety intended to be suitable for the emulation of Christians and, in particular, Christian women. There are no comparable role models in the apocryphal Acts for Christian men. Stratocles, Marcellus, Lycomedes, the various men converted by Paul just before his death, and the others are flawed, only secondary in the narratives, or sketchily developed as narrative characters. The great difficulty in Christian life is said time and time again to be the problem of continent living. This problem is always viewed from the standpoint of a woman who must leave her husband. At no time in the apocryphal Acts does a man encounter substantial difficulties in leaving his wife. Married men are converted to the faith, if at all, either after their wives have converted or simultaneously with their wives.

The episodes previously cited as evidence in this study constitute the great majority of material which survives in reasonably authentic form from the Acts of John, Paul, and Andrew. The Acts of Peter establishes no positive role models forcefully; its thrust is aimed at establishing the negative qualities of Simon Magus. The Acts of Thomas does contain some episodes in which the major characters are male, but those men are usually important because of their opposition to the Christian message. No figure in the Acts of Thomas (except the apostle) is the focus of as much attention as is Mygdonia.

The main thrust of the teachings in those apocryphal Acts we have examined is directed toward women, particularly in the creation of exemplary figures, or role models, for emulation. The difficulty of relating the faith to circumstances is first and foremost expressed as the difficulty married women have in trying to live as continent Christians in the face of opposition from their families. The Acts often present the piety of women not simply as equal to that of men but usually on a higher level. If the intended audience of the apocryphal Acts can be inferred from the overall thrust of the edificatory intent of the Acts, then that audience was Christian women.

The apocryphal Acts are acutely aware of Christians as male and female. Their edificatory intent is directed more to females than to males and, when contrasts are made between the sexes, female Christians are usually shown to be more pious than their male counterparts. From this we can propose with some confidence that the original community of the apocryphal Acts was largely female in composition. Moreover, the women who made up that community were dedicated to a life of continence and eager to urge other women to join that life. They encountered difficulties in their relationships with former husbands and believed that continent Christian women were likely to be more pious than the average Christian man.

To this point in our study we have confined our attention to the Acts of Peter, Paul, John, Andrew, and Thomas, five documents generally considered to date from the mid-second century or early third century. As we demonstrated in the introduction, the Acts of Xanthippe (also known as the Acts of Xanthippe and Polyxena) is another text from that period.

Unlike the other five Acts, the Acts of Xanthippe does not focus on apostles. It is a tale of the tribulations, triumphs, and travels of three women: Xanthippe, Polyxena, and Rebecca. All three are converted to Christianity and beset by lustful men whose advances the women fend off with difficulty. Xanthippe is married, but after her conversion to the faith she refuses to sleep with her husband; the other two women remain virgins. The women are paragons of continent Christian virtue and, while they have thorough understanding of the faith, they are careful not to usurp the apparent masculine prerogative of preaching.

Xanthippe, devoted to Paul, is shown to be capable of elucidating his career for him. After he has mentioned his sufferings, she says to him: "Thou sufferest these things by thy own free will, since thou hast not neglected thy preaching even to scourging but this again I tell thee, that thy bonds shall be the defeat of the prompter, and thy humiliation their overthrow" (A.Xn. 9). The woman here is more than a passive listener, she talks with the apostle as one nearly equal to him. Indeed, having only heard rumors of Christianity she adopts the faith and teaches herself to pray while hoping for Paul's arrival (A.Xn. 3). She never claims equality, however; she is always humble in Paul's presence. Yet she is highly respected. Two wise men come to her saying: "'Pray for us lowly ones, O servant of Christ, that he may bring us also into thy number.' But she said to them, 'Brethren, I am not Paul who remits sins, but neither is he far from you. Therefore fall not before my knees, but go to him, who is also more able to benefit you.'" (A.Xn. 19). Apparently the author of the Acts of Xanthippe knew that women were forbidden to preach to men or absolve and yet believed that women were fully intelligent Christians. Polyxena clarifies a difficulty for a Christian man who asks, "'Does this Paul then have the same God that is preached by Philip?' Polyxena, learning that he was a Christian, said, 'Yea, brother, this is the God of all'" (A.Xn. 31). That this man's problem was one that the author of these Acts found conceivable may indicate an early date for the composition of the work. For our purpose it is significant that a woman here resolves a Christian man's difficulties.

Polyxena and a prefect's son together are thrown to the beasts but, like Thecla, Polyxena is befriended by a lioness. The prefect and the people of the city are astounded.

Seeing this fearful and wonderful sight, (they) gave praise and glory to the merciful God, saying, "Of a truth thou art, and he, that is named by Polyxena, alone is God, for the gods of the heathen are the works of men's hands, unable to save or assist any one. Let them perish now, both themselves and their makers." And the prefect straightway taking his son and Polyxena into the palace, heard from them in order the faith and religion in Christ without omission, and he and all in the city believed, and there was great joy and giving of glory to God. And Polyxena said to the prefect, "Be of good cheer, my lord, for the man of God will quickly come, who will perfectly teach, exhort, instruct, and enlighten you in the knowledge of Christ." (A.Xn. 37)

Perhaps we have here a transformation of the Thecla tale wherein Thecla preached to a queen and a governor. Polyxena also preaches to city authorities, but she is accompanied by an unnamed male.

The focus of attention in the Acts of Xanthippe is on the three women, Rebecca, Polyxena, and Xanthippe. Their virtues and travels are not unlike those of apostles but they are only likened to apostles reservedly. There is no reason to conclude that this reserve stems from any disdain of women. On the contrary, it seems that this document was written at a time and place where preaching by women was forbidden and that Xanthippe, Polyxena, and Rebecca were elevated to the highest level of capability for women short of a claim that women ought to preach. Xanthippe shows a strange ambiguity in speaking of God. She struggles to keep silent but knows that Christ is as much in her as in Paul. Having finally received baptism she says:

> I desire to keep silence, since human reason makes me afraid, lest I have not the grace of eloquence. I desire to keep silence, and am compelled to speak, for some one inflames and sweetens me within. If I say, I will shut my mouth, there is some one that murmurs in me. Shall I say a great thing? Is it not that teacher that is within Paul, without arrogance, filling the heavens speaking within and waiting without, sitting on the throne with the father and stretched out on the cross by man. What, therefore, shall I do I know not. My worthless mind delights me, and is not unfolded to the end (A.Xn. 14).

We know that the author of these Acts is thoroughly familiar with the Thecla sequence in the Acts of Paul.[2] Further, we know that Tertullian railed against the Acts of Paul because therein women were assumed to have the right to preach and to baptize.[3] It is possible that the Acts of Xanthippe is a re-working of the Acts of Paul to retain models of female excellence without wholly flying in the face of church authority. These Acts may have come from a community of women grappling with the demands of male authorities armed with Pauline quotations that they keep silent.

In an incident reflecting the influence of the Acts of Paul, Xanthippe's request for baptism is refused by Paul (A.Xn. 11). In the Acts it is reported that "all this was done by the Evil One that Xanthippe might receive holy baptism with tribulation, and be faint-hearted concerning the commandments of Christ" (A.Xn. 11). Xanthippe may be fainthearted, or frightened, but she never believes in anything but a virtuous fashion. When Xanthippe's husband, Probus, requests baptism he receives it instantly (A.Xn. 21).

2. James, "Acta Xanthippae," pp. 47–51 and p. 53.
3. Tertullian *De Baptismo*, p. 17.

To some extent the Evil One is here seen to be influencing Paul's behavior. As is the case in the Acts of Paul, the apostle, while overtly praised, is subtly criticized for his manner of dealing with women.

On several occasions women put their trust in men to no avail. Philip commends Polyxena to one of his followers, but she is forced to flee from his house after an attack by the forces of a nobleman who loved her (A.Xn. 25). Rebecca and Polyxena turn to an ass-driver for assistance, but he is soon driven away by the servants of a prefect who desires the women (A.Xn. 33). The two women come to the apostle Andrew and plead with him.

"We will follow thee whithersoever thou goest." The Apostle Andrew said, "This was not made known to me by the Lord, daughters; therefore remain with peace, hoping in the Lord, and he will preserve you to the end."
And Andrew went his way rejoicing and glorifying God. Then said Polyxena, "Whither shall we go, sister?" Rebecca said, "Let us depart whether thou wilt, lest my mistress send and separate us." Polyxena said, "Come, let us depart into the mountain to the lioness." Rebecca said, "It is indeed better for us to live with wild beasts and perish of hunger than to be compelled by Greeks and idolators to fall into the filth of marriage" (A.Xn. 30–31).

In this rather poignant little story we can see that, as is evident in the Acts of Paul, holy men were not always seen to be reliable protectors of women.

Rebecca and Polyxena, like Thecla, must rely on their own strength and the aid of God. Rebecca, however, finally finds secure shelter in the home of an aged Christian woman (A.Xn. 35). In both the Acts of Paul and the Acts of Xanthippe women learn not to expect men, even apostles, to assist them but to put their trust in women (Thecla and the queen, Rebecca and the old woman) and in God. At the conclusion of the Thecla sequence, Thecla says: "My God, and God of this house where the light shone upon me, Christ Jesus the Son of God, my helper in prison, my helper before governors, my helper in the fire, my helper among the beasts, thou art God, and to thee be the glory for ever. Amen" (A.Pl. 3:40). Having sought the aid of Paul throughout the entire tale, Thecla at last departs from him and turns to God, realizing that her assistance comes from him, not from an apostle.

While the Acts of Xanthippe seems to discourage women from turning too expectantly to holy men for aid, at the close of the story Polyxena "left not at all the blessed Paul in her fear of temptations" (A.Xn. 42). This ending may well be another attempt by the author of the Acts of Xanthippe to use the Thecla story while moderating it. Thecla's "rebellious" intention to go off on her own and preach is here changed to Polyxena's resolution to stay with Paul.

The Acts of Xanthippe seems particularly relevant to a community largely made up of continent Christian women, for it contains three female figures well established as role models. They are contrasted with rather imperfect male Christians like the ass-driver and the husband of Xanthippe (who becomes Christian only after repeated unsuccessful attempts to resume marital relations with her). Other male Christians are mentioned in passing, but they are always secondary characters. Here, even apostles are secondary. We shall see that the Acts of Xanthippe provides other evidence of its particular concern with women.

While Xanthippe is going up the stairs to her chamber, a demon in the form of an actor approaches her. She takes him for an actor familiar to her and says angrily: "'Many a time have I said to him that I no longer care for toys, and he despises me as being a woman;' and straightway seizing an iron lamp-stand, she hurled it at his face and crushed all his features. Then the demon cried out saying, 'O violence, from this destroyer even women have received power to strike us'" (A.Xn. 21). Christianity is here portrayed as a faith which elevates women and brings them maturity and strength. Xanthippe is shown as capable of defending herself without masculine aid, much to the surprise of her assailant.

The Acts of Xanthippe tells us some of the functions it was intended to serve. At the conclusion of the work, during the reunion of Xanthippe and Polyxena, Xanthippe quotes her husband, Probus, as saying, "It was assigned to her [Polyxena] by God to be thus afflicted. Do you see by how many devices God saves many?" (A.Xn. 41) At least in part, the Acts of Xanthippe appears to have been designed as an explanation for the difficulties continent Christian women encountered in life. At another place in the Acts, the woman Rebecca, having found security in the home of an aged Christian woman, thinks to herself: "Alas, my sister Polyxena, I wretched one did not think that anyone was oppressed like myself, but now I am persuaded and know that all my misfortunes and tribulations do not compare with one day of thine" (A.Xn. 35). Perhaps this was an attitude the author of the Acts of Xanthippe wished to call forth from those who heard that document. In a hymn near the beginning of the Acts, Xanthippe says, "Praise the Lord ye that have despaired like me, for many are his mercies. Alleluia" (A.Xn. 19).

Since the tribulations that occur in the Acts of Xanthippe are tribulations of women, those who were to find their troubles less than those of Polyxena or who, perhaps, were to have despaired like Xanthippe, were themselves probably also women. The exemplary figures set up for emulation in the Acts of Xanthippe are women; from this fact we can argue that the edificatory intention of the Acts was for women.

In the foregoing sections of this study, we have argued that the original community behind the apocryphal Acts was one predominantly composed of continent Christian women. If the Acts did come into being in communities of such women, it may be possible to know more about them than simply their gender. There were, in the early church, established groups of continent women known as widows. We will first establish some facts about the widows in the early orthodox church and then consider the question of whether there is any evidence that the apocryphal Acts were particularly concerned with widows and their problems.

V

Widows and the Apocryphal Acts

CHRISTIANITY, virtually from its outset, took over from Judaism concern for the protection of widows and orphans. Widows soon became an identifiable group in the church, a particular community with shared life-style and shared concerns. This is already evident in the canonical Acts of the Apostles (see Acts 6:1–6 and Acts 9:36–42). First Timothy (5:3–16) is our major source of evidence on widows in the early second century. Charles Ryrie, in writing about First Timothy, says that "the ministry of prayer was expected of all 'widows indeed' regardless of age, and any of the ministries which may be suggested by the text [of Timothy] were not limited to enrolled widows."[1] Further, he says that, "It is evident that widows were accorded a place of honor in the early church and they were the first group of women to be honored in any way as a group."[2]

The term "widow" means then not simply a woman whose husband is deceased, but a particular class of Christian person. In the words of Martin Dibelius, "We are dealing here [in First Timothy] with a gradual technical use of a word that has led to a bureaucratic designation for the 'widows of the community.'"[3] Stählin con-

1. Ryrie, *The Role of Women in the Church*, p. 84.
2. Ibid., p. 85.
3. Quoted in Bangerter, *Frauen im Aufbruch*, p. 41.

cludes from First Timothy that the Greek *chēra katalegésthō* implies a distinct grouping. He writes, "Here and elsewhere *katalégō* means 'to be adopted into a fellowship by election.' The term itself makes it likely that congregational widows already formed a 'semi-clerical' corporation."[4]

In First Timothy we find that "a widow in the full sense, one who is alone in the world, has her hope in God and continues in supplications and prayers night and day" (5:5). Polycarp in his admonitions urges that widows be taught to be "discreet as respects the faith of the Lord, praying constantly for all, being far from all slandering, evil speaking, false witnessing, love of money, and every kind of evil; knowing that they are the altar of God."[5] A widow is expected to conduct herself morally, but her specific duty is constant prayer.

Stählin writes that "According to Ignatius Sm. 13.1 there were virgins who were called widows. Hence virgins could be received into the order of widows, e.g., when there were not enough real widows. Such a case, if extreme, seems to be in view in Tertullian Virg. Vel. 9.2. Often widows are closely associated with virgins, e.g. Tertullian Praescr. Haer., 3, and Hippolytus Ch. Order 23. In the days when widows were no longer ranked as clergy both church widows and *virgines sacratae* seem to have had semi-clerical status."[6] Mary Lawrence McKenna, writing from the information in such sources, believes that "it is most likely that young women and virgins would find the vocation of the widows attractive. It was wide, free, and womanly, useful and honored by the Church. The widows were leaders among the women by example and instruction."[7] It seems clear that the technical term "widow" might often apply to a woman, virgin or widow, particularly dedicated to continence and Christian piety. Indeed, in the words of Roger Gryson: "Christian virgins who resolved to remain chaste 'for the honor of the Lord's flesh' were called 'widows.' Since both groups of women had *a profession of continence as their chief characteristic* their ideals and life-styles seemed similar. In the case of these virgins,

4. Stählin, "Chēra," *Theological Dictionary of the New Testament*, vol. 9, ed. G. Friedrich, p. 456.
5. Polycarp *Ad Phil.* 4.
6. Stählin, "Chēra," p. 464.
7. McKenna, *Women of the Church*, p. 50.

continence most probably went hand in hand with asceticism, prayer and acts of charity; when no close relatives were available, they also, like widows, were assisted by the community." (emphasis added)[8] The term "Encratite" could well be applied to such virgin women.

We can conclude from this brief survey of learned opinion that in the early Christian church continent women, both virgins and widows, were not infrequently grouped under the technical term "widow." Twice in the Acts of Peter (A.Pt. 7:21–22, 8:29) the words "widow" and "virgin" are used to designate the same women. In this study we use "widow" to mean continent Christian women generally, even though in some churches virgins and widows were considered to be in different orders entirely.[9] Widows, many of whom were probably elderly (see First Timothy 5:9), had the special office of constant prayer both day and night. They also seem to have played an important role in ministering to Christian women. The community was responsible for the financial support of those widows who had no other resources on which to rely.

One further fact is worthy of mention: Widows were women who had a special bond to Christ, one like the bond of marriage. Stählin makes this clear in his comment on the term *memonōmenē*, which is found in First Timothy (5:5). "The added *kaì memonōménē* is to be understood as an interpretation of *ē ŏntōs chēra*, the widow who really stands alone, who has no relatives to whom she is under obligation. The concept of the *ŏntōs chēra kaì memonōménē* obviously includes, however, another feature, namely that she is determined not to engage in a fresh marriage. The decisive thing here is not whether she is, or feels, too old for this. What counts is the resolve *memonōsthai* and therewith, as implied in v. 12, to enter into a special bond with Christ."[10] The status of widowhood, then, implies a pledge of continence, a resolution to be faithful to Christ rather than to a partner in an earthly marriage.

8. Gryson, *The Ministry of Women in the Early Church*, p. 13.
9. See Ryrie, for support (following Lightfoot) of the view that in the orthodox church, "in Ignatius' time there was a recognized order of widows who were really widows and not virgins, just as was the case in the Pastorals" (*The Role of Women in the Church*, p. 99). The likelihood is that in some places there were two groups, virgins and widows, and in other places but one.
10. Stählin, "Chēra," p. 456.

"Widows" were a group which could at times include both widows and virgins; widows were continent, often dependent upon the church for financial support, often of advanced age, expected to pray constantly, and resolved to remain faithful to Christ. Such a group of women would have had a collective identity, even a semiclerical status. Widows would have been substantially concerned that the church have the financial capacity and willingness to provide them sustenance. A church that could provide for such a group of dependent women would have to be one with a reasonably well-organized social structure such that funds might be solicited, collected, administered, and disbursed efficiently and fairly. Indeed, it is an intent of the letter First Timothy to outline a church hierarchy such that fiduciary support could be efficiently provided to widows and that only destitute widows might receive financial support.

If those who were the original community behind the apocryphal Acts were primarily continent Christian women, as we have argued in the previous chapter, then it is possible that they were women who identified themselves as widows. The widows we may find in the Acts would include women who are virgins or widows or women who have separated from their husbands by choice. They would in that way be somewhat different from the widows known to us from most other early Christian literature wherein women were encouraged (if not required) to maintain their marital ties. If the community behind the Acts was composed largely of widows, we will expect to find widows, and elderly women, approvingly mentioned and their concerns dealt with in the context of the Acts. We have already seen that continence was a main characteristic of the women held up for emulation in the Acts. We will proceed to look for indications that the Acts are concerned with the financial well-being of Widows and then for evidence that widows and apostles were said to have had a particularly close relationship.

The Acts of Paul, in a fragmentary portion, reports that Paul visits the city of Myra and raises up a father and his son. The father, a committed Christian, sold his possessions and "brought the price to the widows" (A.Pl. 4). Similarly, in the Acts of Peter it is reported that:

Peter had arranged to go to Marcellus on the Lord's day, to see the widows as Marcellus had promised, so that they should be cared for by his own hands. So the boy who had returned to life said, "I will not leave Peter." And his mother went joyfully and gladly to her own house. And on the next day after the Sabbath she came to Marcellus' house bringing Peter two thousand pieces of gold and saying to Peter, "Divide these among the virgins of Christ who serve him." But when the boy who had risen from the dead saw that he had given nothing to anyone, he went home and opened the chest and himself brought four thousand gold pieces (A.Pt. 8:29).

The widows mentioned here are not merely destitute women; they are a particular group of Christians with a collective identity, the "virgins of Christ who serve him."

On another occasion in those Acts another woman whose son has been raised declares that she will give some of her property to newly freed slaves. The apostle Peter immediately says to her, "Let the remainder be distributed to the widows" (A.Pt. 8:28).

Such concern for the financial well-being of widows is even more evident in the Acts of Thomas. There a woman delivers a lengthy discourse on a vision which recently she has had of hell and of the Devil, a black man (A.Th. 6:55). The apostle then delivers a homily, and "all the people believed, and yielded their souls obedient to the living God and to Christ Jesus, rejoicing in the blessed works of the Most High and in his holy service. And they brought much money for the service of the widows; for he had them gathered together in the cities, and to them all he sent what was necessary by his deacons, both clothing and provision for their nourishment. But he himself did not cease preaching and speaking to them and showing that this is Jesus the Christ whom the Scriptures proclaimed" (A.Th. 6:59). Here we can see that the community behind the Acts was quite concerned that widows be well provided for. Further, widows are "gathered together" into communities, suggesting concern for widows as an identifiable collectivity, not for widows as an example of poor people in general.

The Acts of John shows an acute awareness of the difficulties of aged women, to the apparent exclusion of aged men's difficulties.

He [John] commanded Verus, the brother who attended him, to bring the old women (that were) in the whole of Ephesus and he and Cleopatra and Lycomedes made preparations to care for them. So Verus came and said to John, "Out of the old women over sixty that are here I have found only four in good bodily health; of the others (some are . . .) and some paralytic and others sick."

And John on hearing this kept silence for a long time then he rubbed his face and said, "Oh, what slackness among the people of Ephesus! What a collapse, what weakness towards God! O devil, what a mockery you have made all this time of the faithful at Ephesus! Jesus who gives me grace and the gift of confidence in him, says to me now in silence, 'Send for the old women who are sick, and be with them in the theater and through me heal them'" (A.Jn. 30).

After a long harangue against the men of Ephesus, John heals all the women's diseases. It is significant that the "faithful" are accused of laxity in neglecting elderly women. This passage seems to be a complaint written by Christians criticizing Christians for neglect of a particular group of Christians, women over sixty. This age is exactly that specified in First Timothy for enrollment in the order of widows.

A section of the Acts of Peter shows even more dramatically the concern of an apostle for a group of widows. We see there that widows are for a time closeted with the apostle, that they have visions of Christ, and that their financial worries are relieved.

Marcellus, a Christian man formerly deceived by Simon Magus, returns to the faith and addresses Peter: "Now, most blessed man, I have told the widows and the aged to meet you in my house which is cleansed, that they may pray with us. And each of them shall be given a piece of gold on account of their service, so that they may truly be called Christ's servants" (A.Pt. 7:19). Soon afterwards Peter returns sight to a blind widow and delivers a lengthy discourse regarding his own vision of Christ who is "both great and little, beautiful and ugly, young and old" etc. (A.Pt. 7:20). Thereafter a number of "old blind widows" ask to be healed. Peter agrees to return their sight to them and says: "'Yet now, Lord, let your sweet and holy name assist these women; do thou touch their eyes for thou art able that they may see with their own eyesight.' And then prayer was made by all, the room in which they were shone as if with lightning, such as shines in the clouds. Yet it was not such light as (is seen) by day, (but) ineffable, invisible such as no man could describe. . . . And as we lay there, there stood there only those widows, which were blind. But the bright light which appeared to us entered into their eyes and made them see" (A.Pt. 7:21).

The widows subsequently, at Peter's request, describe their experience as a vision of the Lord who to some was an old man, to others a growing boy, to others a child. Peter responds: "'So, brethren, as I told you a little while ago, God is greater than our thoughts, as we have learned from the aged widows, how they have seen the Lord in a variety of forms.' And he exhorted them all to understand the Lord with all their heart; then he and Marcellus and the other brethren began to attend to the virgins of the Lord and to rest until morning. Marcellus said to them, 'You holy and inviolate virgins of the Lord, give ear; you have a place where you (may) stay. For the things that are called mine to whom do they belong but to you?'" (A.Pt. 7:21–22) This account is one of the lengthiest and most detailed reports of a vision of Christ in the Acts, a vision beheld by widows who are also called the virgins of the Lord.

The Acts repeatedly acknowledge that pious and continent women could receive apparitions of the Lord. Drusiana, Mygdonia, Thecla, Maximilla, and Iphidamia see visions of Christ, or Christ in the form of an apostle. Xanthippe has a vision, reported in detail, of the Lord arriving in thunder and glory but, out of pity, changing into the likeness of Paul so that she might not be terrified (A.Xn. 15). Xanthippe, Drusiana, Maximilla, Iphidamia, and Mygdonia have their visions when they are not in the company of men. In the Acts of Peter the widows see a vision from which the men who are present are excluded. The widows' visions of Christ are soon followed by a contrasting vision beheld by Marcellus who sees the Devil in the form of a black woman (A.Pt. 7:22). Marcellus's vision forms an interesting contrast with the vision of a woman in the Acts of Thomas who sees the Devil as a black man (A.Th. 6:55). In the Acts of Thomas one man sees Christ in the form of Thomas; but this man is accompanied by his new bride, and she is the focal point of the story (A.Th. 1:11). On the whole, the apocryphal Acts either indicate that visions of the Lord were more part of the Christian experience of continent women than of Christian men, or that the compilers of the Acts were not very much concerned with the visions beheld by men.

The passage in the Acts of Peter quoted on the previous page shows Peter in close contact with widows; something similar is present in the Acts of Paul. A mother whose son has been newly converted to the faith "took his hand and brought (him) to the widows and Paul" (A.Pl. 4). This section of the Acts is too fragmentary for us to know how "the widows and Paul" came to be together. When Thecla in the Acts of Paul first hears the apostle, she desires to go to him: "moreover, when she saw many women and virgins going in to Paul she desired to be counted worthy herself to stand in Paul's presence and hear the word of Christ" (A.Pl. 3:7). Apparently these women were not just curious passersby but Christians "worthy" to come in to Paul. The Acts of Paul, like the Acts of Peter and John and Thomas, shows widows gathered together as a recognized collectivity. The two authentic segments of the Acts of Andrew that remain mention no widows, but do contain a report of a virgin sister who receives a vision of Christ. The Acts of Xanthippe likewise has no mention of widows; however, Rebecca finds permanent safety in the dwelling of an elderly Christian woman.

Most of the apocryphal Acts show specific concern for the health and financial security of widows over and above a general concern for the poor and weak. We have not thought it wise, incidentally, to adduce as evidence instances in the Acts of the cliché that "widows and orphans" should be cared for. Widows in the Acts are gathered together and are shown to be capable of visionary experience. Apathy on the part of Christians in caring for their difficulties is reproved. The very establishment of communities of widows is given apostolic sanction in the Acts of Thomas. We can conclude that there were communities of widows known to the composers of the Acts and that the Acts show intense respect for such communities.

The existence of organized groups of continent, predominantly elderly, dependent women requires there to be a well-organized social and financial apparatus to support them. Those churches which had dependent groups of widows also had a church organization composed of some or all of the offices known to have existed in the second-century Christian church: deacon, presbyter, bishop. Yet these offices are hardly ever mentioned in the Acts, and when they are it is usually in a haphazard manner. It will be possible to discuss all the occurrences of words denoting church offices in a short space.

No church offices are mentioned in the Acts of Paul or in the Acts of John. None are mentioned in the Acts of Xanthippe or in the surviving sections of the Acts of Andrew. In the Acts of Peter we hear of a single church official, Narcissus the presbyter. Of all the men in the Roman church only he did not become an adherent of Simon Magus. He is not the only Christian person to remain loyal, however, being joined in his fidelity by "two women in the lodging-house of the Bithynians and four who could no longer go out of their house; and being thus confined they devoted themselves to prayer day and night" (A.Pt. 2:4). These latter four are identifiably widows, for they are both aged and engaged in prayer "day and night," the duty First Timothy advocates for widows. One man and six women remain loyal: a presbyter, four widows, and two other women.

At one other place in the Acts of Peter church offices are mentioned. The apostle Peter seeks to raise up a dead boy and says: "Lord, give light, appear, and raise up the son of this aged widow who cannot help herself without her son. Now I take up the word of Christ my master, and say to thee, Young man, arise and walk with thy mother, so long as thou art useful to her. But afterwards thou shalt offer thyself to me in a higher service, in the office of deacon and bishop" (A.Pt. 8:27). The boy, of course, is successfully raised. Peter makes it quite clear, however, that his duties to his widowed mother take precedence over any future role in the church hierarchy.

In the Acts of Thomas we find church officials mentioned more than once. Thomas intends to baptize a woman whom he has just exorcised (A.Th. 5:49). He commands his servant (deacon) to set up a table before them. In another place (A.Th. 6:59) the apostle sends his servants (deacons) to gather widows together and provide for them (A.Th. 6:59). At the conclusion of the Acts of Thomas two men, Siphor and Vazan, are appointed to church office (A.Th. Mart. 169). In these instances church offices are mentioned only in passing. Once, however, Thomas chooses a deacon with considerable fanfare. The people are gathered together and Thomas discourses to them: "I am now going from you, and it is uncertain whether I shall see you again according to the flesh. . . . But I leave with you Xenophon the deacon in my place, for he also preaches Jesus, even as I do. For neither am I anything, nor is he, but Jesus. For indeed I too am a man clothed with a body, a son of man like one of you" (A.Th. 7:66). There is nothing particularly remarkable about this passage in the Acts of Thomas except that it is unique. We expect, in tales of apostles, for those apostles to establish successors, to institute officers of the church in the towns they visit. This happens only this once with any emphasis whatsoever.

Whoever the community behind the Acts were, they were people who were *not* concerned with the problems and legitimacy and virtues of church officials. However, they had substantial concern for widows, virgins of Christ, and aged women, people who were dependent upon a stable church structure for financial support. If the apocryphal Acts were written by or for officials of the church, then these officials were so modest, so little concerned with their own legitimacy and difficulties, so willing to resist the temptation to insert mention of their own offices in their documents that one can but stand in awe of their humility. Nothing of second- and early third-century Christian literature indicates that officials of the church did other than pride themselves on their position and authority. The striking absence of concern in the Acts for church officialdom argues against any notion that they were composed by men holding high position in a church. It is far more likely that the apocryphal Acts derive from people who were not themselves church officials and who felt no inclination to discuss church officials.

The community behind the Acts exhibits through the Acts its great concern for widows, virgins, and aged women. The existence of such financially dependent women rules out the conclusion that the absence of evidence for a stably organized church means that such a church did not exist in the lives of the people responsible for the Acts. We can only conclude that such a financially competent church did exist, but that those who compiled the Acts were not concerned to write about it.

From both positive and negative evidence, we are led to the conclusion that the community behind the Acts was largely composed of continent Christian women. It seems likely that those women often identified themselves as widows.

If a considerable portion of the original community behind the Acts was composed of women who were separated from their husbands by choice, as the Acts lead us to believe, then we would expect to find their experiences of separation reflected in the Acts. Such experiences appear in sections of the Acts that feature spurned husbands pleading with their newly continent wives for the resumption of normal marital relations. These are remarkable passages for, while these same husbands are characterized in the narratives as tyrannical persons, their speeches to their wives are often reasonable and even tender.

The proconsul Aegeates, elsewhere described by the apostle Andrew as "a corrupter, deceiver, destroyer, a madman, a magician, a cheat, a murderer, wrathful," etc. (A.An. Narr. 34), speaks to his wife, Maximilla, who has recently been converted to a life of Christian continence:

Thy parents, Maximilla, considered me worthy of marriage with you, and gave you to me as wife, looking neither to wealth nor family nor renown, but perhaps (only) to the good character of my soul. And intending to pass over much with which I wished to reproach you, both things which I have enjoyed from your parents and things which you (enjoyed) from me during all our life together, I have come from the court to learn this alone from you; answer me reasonably: if you were the person you used to be, living with me in the way we know, sleeping with me, keeping up marital intercourse with me, bearing my children, then I would treat you well in everything; even more, I would release the stranger whom I have in prison (A.An. Cod. Vat. 4).

Perhaps we can hear in his speech to his wife very much the sort of thing that was said to newly continent Christian women. He refers to his fondness for her, restrains his temptation to reproach her, and urges her to consider that her parents selected him for her because of their trust in his character. Maximilla, nevertheless, rejects him.

A similar speech is put in the mouth of the ruler Charisius in the Acts of Thomas when he encounters his wife Mygdonia who has just become Christian and separated from him:

He found her with (her hair shorn) and her garments rent. And seeing this he said to her: "My lady Mygdonia, why does this cruel sickness hold thee fast? And why has thou done these things? I am thy husband from thy virginity, and both the gods and the laws give me (the right) to rule over thee. What is this great madness of thine, that thou art become a laughing-stock in all our nation? . . . They are taking away my soul, and the beautiful body in which I rejoiced when I saw it they are destroying; the sharpest of eyes they are blinding, and they are cutting off my right hand. My joy is turned to grief and my life to death, and the light (is plunged) in darkness. . . . My lady, most beloved Mygdonia, remember that out of all the women in India I chose thee as the fairest and took thee, when I could have joined to myself in marriage others far more beautiful than thee. . . . If thou wilt be with me, such as thou wast before thou didst see that sorcerer, I will do all thy desires, and if because of thy friendship for him thou shouldst wish it, I will take him out of the prison and set him free, and he may go to another country. And I will not vex thee, for I know that thou art greatly attached to the stranger. And it was not with thee first that this matter came about, but he has also deceived many other women along with thee. But they have come to their senses and returned to themselves" (A.Th. 9:114–16).

This lengthy discourse contains a number of themes which might have been matters of real concern to men abandoned by their wives. The husband is here concerned for his wife's health and sanity and worried also that he not be made a laughingstock. He says that he finds his wife beautiful; although not the most beautiful woman in the nation, she was his personal choice for a wife. The apostle he finds to be a sorcerer, interrupting the normal relationships of society, and yet he offers not to revenge himself upon his wife's new friend if only she will return to him. It is interesting to note that the concluding phrases of the speech imply that the apostle is having an effect primarily, if not exclusively, on women.

Mygdonia does not return, and at the end of the Acts of Thomas Charisius and another man, Misdaeus, .whose wife had also left him, (A.Th. Mart. 169), "being unable to persuade them [their wives] allowed them to live according to their own will" (A.Th. Mart. 169). Most speeches in the Acts are either theological discourses or savage imprecations. The speeches of these two husbands in the Acts of Thomas and Andrew are strikingly, if not uniquely, realistic. We can easily suppose that they are just the sort of thing shocked and confused husbands might say to newly Christian and newly continent wives.

Spurned husbands do not always act so calmly in the apocryphal Acts, as they must have not always acted so calmly in reality. In a lost portion of the Acts of John, which is alluded to later in the narrative, the woman Drusiana is locked by her husband in a tomb because of her insistence on chastity (A.Jn. 63). In the Acts of Peter Albinus, whose wife has left him, is reported to have reacted violently: "He, therefore, filled with fury and passionate love for Xanthippe, and amazed that she would not even sleep in the same bed with him, was raging like a wild beast . . ." (A.Pt. 9:34). In the Acts of Xanthippe, Probus, Xanthippe's husband, becomes a Christian because he is so anxious to avoid the humiliation sure to follow from the fact that his wife has deserted him. He says: "Alas, how wretched was the day in which I was wedded to Xanthippe. Would that I had died and not seen her. Saying this he arose and said, I shall pray to the God of Paul. Perchance he will do to me also what is fitting, that I may not become a reproach in the world, being rejected by her" (A.Xn. 20). Like Charisius, Probus is worried that his wife's rejection of him will make him a laughingstock.

It seems reasonable to conclude from such passages that the community behind the apocryphal Acts was one quite sensitive to the emotional difficulties inherent in the separation of wives from their husbands. Judging by their moderate tone, we can surmise that the speeches directed to newly continent wives cited above reflect the sort of discourses that some Christian women might have had directed to them in their own lives—if their husbands or fiancés were moderate men. Reactions of outrage must also have occurred from men of a different temperament, when their wives became adherents of strange ascetic wonder workers. Never in the apocryphal Acts does a husband suffer the reproaches of his wife when he becomes a Christian.

If the community behind the Acts was mainly composed of continent Christians, we should not be surprised to find passages in the Acts which are comprehensible only in such a context. Two events reported in the Acts of Peter seem to be theodicies relevant only to such a community. Peter on one occasion half paralyzes his own daughter (A.Pt. Frag. a). One another occasion God, after Peter's request, strikes dead a young girl (A.Pt. Frag. b). The daughter is stricken to prevent her from being married. The young girl perishes because Peter had prayed to the Lord to "bestow upon her what was expedient for her soul." At her father's request, however, she is raised from the dead only to run off with a young man.

In both cases the seeming disasters are supposed to be for the best because they prevent the possibility of sexual intercourse. Bizarre as these stories are, they do make some sense as ways of rationalizing paralysis and early death in the context of a community of continent women.

To climax our argument we will quote Evodius of Uzala who preserves a fragment of the Acts of Andrew. "When Maximilla and Iphidamia went away together to hear the Apostle Andrew a handsome little boy, whom Leucius took to be either God or at least an angel, handed them over to the Apostle Andrew; and he departed to the Praetorium of Egetes, went into the bedroom and imitated a woman's voice, as if Maximilla were complaining about the suffering of the female sex and Iphidamia were answering her. When Egetes heard this conversation he believed that they were within and went away." [11] It certainly is a shame that this apocryphal discourse of Christ the *puerulus speciosus* has not been handed down to us. Nonetheless, that there ever was such a discourse at all is further evidence that the Acts were composed within a community that was largely female. We shall see that this community probably saw themselves as brides of Christ and that this self-image is related to the very literary form of the apocryphal Acts.

In several of the Acts available to us sexual continence is urged because Christians are pledged to marriage with Christ. The Acts of John (as reported in the apocryphal Epistle of Titus), after listing in clause after clause metaphors likening earthly marriage to utter disaster, goes on to say, "Hearing this, my children, bind yourselves each one of you in an indivisible, true and holy matrimony, waiting for the one incomparable and true bridegroom from heaven, even Christ, who is a bridegroom forever." [12] This notion is echoed in the Acts of Thomas where "the Lord Jesus in the like-

---

11. Schneemelcher and Hennecke, eds., *New Testament Apocrypha*, pp. 402–3.
12. Ibid., p. 210.

ness of the apostle Judas Thomas" tells a new bride to anticipate the
"incorruptible and true marriage" (A.Th. 1:12). A little later the
bride, having decided to live continently, tells her father that: "I
have set at naught this man, and this marriage, which passes away
from before my eyes, because I am bound in another marriage.
And that I have had no intercourse with a short-lived husband, the
end of which is (remorse and bitterness) of soul, (is) because I am
yoked with the true man" (A.Th. 1:14). At another place in the
Acts of Thomas we find the same theme. Mygdonia's husband asks
her to return to him and she replies: "Thou hast seen that marriage,
which passed away (and remains here on earth), but this marriage
abides for ever. That fellowship was one of corruption, but this of
life eternal. Those attendants are short-lived men and women, but
these now remain to the end. That bridal chamber is taken down,
but this remains for ever. That bed was spread with coverlets, but
this with love and faith. Thou art a bridegroom who passes away
and is destroyed but Jesus is a true bridegroom, abiding immortal
for ever" (A.Th. 10:124). In the Acts of Xanthippe again we find
the same idea. The heroine Polyxena is approached by a young man
and fears that he will attack her. He, however, says "I do not seek
to be wedded with thee as the bridegroom of destruction, for I
know from thy prayer that thou art the bride of the God of heaven"
(A.Xn. 36). From these indications we can conclude that the idea of
the continent Christian woman as the bride of Christ was a familiar
one to the community from which the apocryphal Acts originated.

  Life-styles are often dictated by people's ruling metaphoric system; in the Acts we find a life-style closely related to a metaphorical
view of salvation, for example, that to be saved one must strive to
remain fit for marital union with Christ. The primitive Christian
metaphor of the bride and the bridegroom seems to have been
taken quite literally by the community behind the Acts. Whether
the ideal Christian is thought to be married on earth to Christ or
betrothed to a future celestial bridegroom is unclear, but in either
case the implications for behavior are the same. If one's religious life
is predicated on the notion that one is related to Christ as a bride is
related to her bridegroom, then one must oppose the advances of
all other suitors, even those with whom one has contracted an
"earthly" marriage. Marital and extramarital intercourse become
equally adulterous. The central value which emerges is one of fidel-

ity, or negatively stated, the avoidance of adultery. This chief value also underlies the dramatic structure of ancient Hellenistic love romances. Söder concludes that of the possible types of romances, that of the love romance is most like the Acts.

How great is the relationship [of the Acts] to the romance is evidenced by the decidedly typical traits which are almost always employed: constant mention of beauty, love at first sight, repudiation of the first and socially approved lover, change of garments, the jealousy and laments of love of the abandoned lover, visits to jail with the attempt to bribe the guards, the motifs of rejected love which turns to hate and expresses itself (a) against the previous beloved or (b) against the rival; the motifs of delay and subterfuge, steadfastness against flattery, threat and even resistance against brutal violence, faithful slaves, etc.

Out of these *topoi*, each of which is employed by ancient love romances, are built the erotic tales in the apocryphal Acts.[13]

This odd connection between teasingly erotic love romances and ascetic apocryphal Acts has a rather simple explanation. Soder hints at this explanation when she writes that, "In the apocryphal Acts we find the same ascetic teachings and the idea of chastity at work as in the novel. But in the novel this applies only to the time of separation, whereas in the apocryphal Acts it is the absolute and only goal."[14] The continent life was not however an absolute goal for those who wrote and heard the Acts; it was a temporary situation meant to prevail on earth in a condition of separation from the bridegroom Christ. The real goal was union with Christ.

The fundamental metaphor of bride and bridegroom implies the fundamental value of continence; the bride owes physical fidelity to the bridegroom. The continent life is one predicated on the separation of a loving couple who seek each other. The love romance as a form of literature is, as we have seen, similarly predicated.

We can envision behind the apocryphal Acts a community of widows who take very seriously the fundamental metaphor of bride and bridegroom. This dominant metaphor was lived out in a continent form of life, one which found all marital and extramarital intercourse to be equally unfaithful and adulterous. We have al-

13. Söder, *Die apokryphen Apostelgeschichten*, p. 148.
14. Ibid., p. 116.

ready seen that, according to Stählin, the widows of the orthodox church had a special bond with Christ, which precluded marriage.[15] Tertullian mentions that those women who practice continence "prefer to be wedded to God."[16] Whether the metaphor preceded the life-style or the life-style was vindicated by creation of a metaphoric justification can never be known. Whatever the case may have been, the love romance was found to be a particularly suitable form to narrate the adventures of the charismatic leaders who preached continent adherence to the bride-bridegroom metaphor. A way of life (continence), a fundamental religious metaphor (bride-bridegroom), and a type of literature (the love romance) form a self-consistent unity in the apocryphal Acts.

The fact that the Acts are very much like ancient love romances is directly relevant to our argument that the Acts are intended for a predominantly female audience. In his classic work, *Der griechische Roman*, Erwin Rohde states that, "Indeed the character of just that part of Hellenistic fiction with which we are dealing here can only be completely explained if we take it as being first and foremost *intended for women*" (Rohde's emphasis).[17] If the ancient romance was a form of writing that appealed primarily to a female audience, the apocryphal Acts modeled on such romances would have appealed to a similar audience.

The value of a hypothesis can be determined by how well it accounts for otherwise puzzling facts. The hypothesis that the Acts derive from communities primarily composed of continent female Christians accounts for the extraordinary emphasis on sexual continence found in the Acts and for the fact that the Acts feature female Christians as role models. This hypothesis also accounts for

15. Stählin, "Chēra," p. 456.
16. Tertullian *Ad Uxorem* 4.
17. Rohde, *Der griechische Roman und seine Vorläufer*, p. 67; see also Karl Schmidt, who writes: "When one finds in the apocryphal Acts lengthy stories concerning sexual asceticism, one is always reminded of those Hellenistic erotic stories about which Erwin Rohde wrote in his book on the Greek novel. In the laments of disappointed lovers, fiancés, and husbands, as well as in the representation of their passions, a clear dependence on such erotic literature is evident." (*Kanonische und apokryphe Evangelien und Apostelgeschichten*, pp. 87–88). F. F. Abbott also believes women to have been the ancient novel's primary audience and cites the "lady pupils" of Horace's day and the literary women of Juvenal's diatribe (*Society and Politics in Ancient Rome*, p. 87).

the great concern shown for the financial, spiritual, and physical well-being of widows, and for the total lack of concern for the problems of bishops, presbyters, and deacons. Finally, it allows us to attribute the fact that women are often favorably contrasted with men to a positive self-image on the part of Christian women rather than to a negative self-image on the part of Christian men. If we hypothesize that the Acts come from communities composed to a great extent of continent Christian women, then the edificatory purposes evident in the Acts, the stress on widows in the Acts, and even, perhaps, the literary genre on which the Acts are modeled come together into a comprehensible pattern.

The social situation in the Acts appears to have been triangular, composed of charismatic apostles, communities of continent women, and Christian men whose authority stemmed from the legitimacy of office. Since the latter, as we have seen, are very seldom mentioned in the Acts, we assumed that the male hierarchy of the church interacted rather infrequently with the widows. An examination of the two Epistles of Pseudo-Clement on virginity will help clarify the relationship between widows and the continent male officials of the church.[18]

These documents derive from a community which, like that behind the apocryphal Acts, placed very high value on sexual continence. According to J. B. Lightfoot, "the Epistles to Virgins can hardly have been written before the middle of the second century. At the same time they bear the stamp of antiquity and in the opinion of some competent writers (e.g. Westcott *Canon* pg. 162, Hefele in Wetzer u. Welte's *Kirchen-Lexicon II* pg. 586) cannot be placed much later than that date. Neander (*Church History* 1, p. 408. Bohn's trans.) places them 'in the last times of the second or in the third century.' As they seem to have emanated from Syria, and the Syrian Church changed less rapidly than the Greek or the Western, it is safer to relax the limits of the possible date to the third century."[19] Lightfoot states further that "the existing Syriac text is doubtless a translation from a Greek original, as the phenomena of the letters themselves suggest."[20] The Epistles seem to come from a Greek-

18. Riddle, trans., "Two Epistles Concerning Virginity," in *The Ante-Nicene Christian Fathers*, vol. 8, ed. A. Roberts and J. Donaldson.

19. J. B. Lightfoot, *The Apostolic Fathers, Part One*, vol. I, p. 407.

20. Ibid., p. 412.

speaking region not very far from Syria and from a time shortly after the middle of the second century. For these reasons and because they place very high value on sexual continence, they seem to stem from the same region, time, and milieu of ideas as the apocryphal Acts. However, and this is most significant for our argument, the relationship between men and women advocated by the Epistles is strikingly *different* from the one evidenced in the Acts.

Pseudo-Clement uses the terms "virgin" and "maiden" to denote women pledged to a life of Christian continence. The greeting in his First Epistle is to "the blessed brother virgins, who devote themselves to preserve virginity 'for the sake of the kingdom of heaven'; and to the holy sister virgins; the peace which is in God" (1 Epistle 1). His Second Epistle is largely devoted to instruction of male virgins in their relations with female virgins. Speaking of his own town, he writes: "With maidens we do not dwell, nor have we anything in common with them; with maidens we do not eat, nor drink; and, where a maiden sleeps, we do not sleep; neither do women wash our feet, nor anoint us; and on no account do we sleep where a maiden sleeps who is unmarried or has taken the vow" (2 Epistle 1). In a town where both men and women are present, the leaders to whom Pseudo-Clement addresses himself should

serve the brethren, and each one of the brethren who are in the same place will join with him in rendering all those services which are requisite for the brethren. But with us may no female, whether young maiden or married woman, be there at that time; [lit. "will with him minister all those things" Riddle] nor she that is aged, nor she that has taken the vow; not even a maid-servant, whether Christian or heathen; but there shall only be men with men. And, if we see it to be requisite to stand and pray for the sake of the women, and to speak words of exhortation and edification, we call together the brethren and all the holy sisters and maidens, and likewise all the other women who are there, inviting them with all modesty and becoming behavior to come and feast on the truth. And those among us who are skilled in speaking speak to them, and exhort them in those words which God has given us. And then we pray, and salute one another, the men the men. But the women and the maidens will wrap their hands in their garments; and we also, with circumspection and with all purity, our eyes looking upwards; and then they will come and give us the salutation on our right hand wrapped in our garments (2 Epistle 1).

Although the men of Pseudo-Clement's community had some regard for women, they sought to avoid even the slightest physical contact with them. The few duties of such Christian men to Christian women are clear: "We address to them [female virgins] words of exhortation in the fear of God and read the scripture to them with purity and in the concise and weighty words of the fear of God" (2 Epistle 4). For Pseudo-Clement women are the greatest threat to man's salvation, yet it is the function of the leaders of the religious community to minister to them. His ambivalent attitude is strikingly clear in the following passage: "But if, moreover, we chance upon a place, and find there one believing woman only, and no other person be there but she only, we do not stop there, nor pray there, nor read the Scriptures there, but we flee as from before the face of a serpent, and as from before the face of sin. Not that we disdain the believing woman, far be it from us to be so minded towards our brethren in Christ!" (2 Epistle 5) This community leader is willing to forgo his normal duties of praying and Scripture reading for fear of the simple physical proximity of a woman. He cautions his followers that: "We do not allow any man whatsoever to sit with a married woman; much less to live in the same house with a maiden who has taken the vow, or to sleep where she sleeps, or to be constantly with her. For this is to be hated and abominated by those who fear God" (2 Epistle 9). He is not saying that sexual intercourse is an abomination (this is assumed); what is to be loathed and hated is for continent Christian men to be near to women at all, except for structured occasions of Scripture reading and exhortation.

Pseudo-Clement has a vision of what the apostles were like, just as do the authors of the apocryphal Acts, but in one key respect his vision is the opposite of theirs.

But see what it [Scripture] says also concerning those holy men, the prophets, and concerning the apostles of our Lord. Let us see whether any one of these holy men was constantly with maidens, or with young married women, or with such widows as the divine apostle declines to receive. Let us consider, in the fear of God, the manner of life of these holy men. Lo! we find it written concerning Moses and Aaron, that they acted and lived in the company of men, who themselves also followed a course of conduct like theirs. And thus did Joshua also, the son of Nun. Woman was there none with them; but they by themselves used holily to minister before God, men with men (2 Epistle 14).

Our Lord Himself was constantly with His twelve disciples when He had come forth to the world. And not only so; but also, when He was sending them out, He sent them out two and two together, men with men; but women were not sent with them, and neither in the highway nor in the house did they associate with women or with maidens: and thus they pleased God in everything (2 Epistle 15).

The apocryphal Acts and these Epistles represent the relationship between apostles and Christian women in diametrically opposite ways. The Acts show the apostles in constant proximity to women; Pseudo-Clement claims that they kept strictly apart from women. The Acts repeatedly show apostles "constantly with maidens, or with young married women, or with . . . widows" and claim that women associated with apostles on highways and in houses. In showing this the Acts do *not* simply repeat Christian tradition; they make a claim about the apostles of the Lord that at least some contemporary continent Christian men absolutely rejected.

The author of the Epistles is clearly a man of authority submitting instructions to his subordinates. He and other men have a preaching role in the community of maidens and virgins who have taken the vow. In his Christian community he has authority over both men and women, an authority which does not stem from charismatic performance but from a structured church. He is not itinerant but firmly rooted in a particular place where both groups of continent Christian women and various continent church leaders with authority over them are present. The men remain as aloof as possible from the women without fully giving up the function of preaching and reading "weighty words of the fear of God" to them.

The Epistles also hint that itinerant wonder-working Christian preachers were present in their society, men like the apostles of whom we wrote in Chapter 3. Pseudo-Clement writes angrily about "reports concerning shameless men who, under pretext of the fear of God, have their dwelling with maidens, and so expose themselves to danger" (1 Epistle 10). It is interesting that these men who associate with women, in even Pseudo-Clement's judgment, do so not from lust but from the fear of God. A little later he adds that they "eat and drink with them [maidens] at entertainments allowing themselves in loose behavior and much uncleanness—such as ought not to be among believers, and especially among those who have chosen for themselves a life of holiness" (1 Epistle 10). At the minimum a "life of holiness" means that the believers Pseudo-Clement disdains are pledged to sexual continence. He states that they "gad about among the houses of virgin brethren or sisters, on pretence of visiting them, or reading the Scriptures to them, or exorcising them. . . . they are idle and do no work, they pry into those things which ought not to be inquired into" (1 Epistle 10).

According to Pseudo-Clement, these men emphasize exorcism quite strongly and "visit those who are harassed by evil spirits and pray and pronounce adjurations over them." They do so "with a multitude of fine words, well prepared and arranged, so that they may appear to men eloquent and of a good memory. Such men are 'like a sounding pipe, or a tinkling cymbal'; and they bring no help to those over whom they make their adjurations; but they speak with terrible words, and affright people" (1 Epistle 12). Pseudo-Clement does not oppose exorcism, but he wants it to be done quietly. The sick ought to be visited, "in a way that is right, without guile, and without covetousness, and without noise, and without talkativeness, and without such behavior as is alien from the fear of God, and without haughtiness, but with the meek and lowly spirit of Christ" (1 Epistle 12). His would be dull exorcisms indeed in contrast with those of his opponents, who are not only flamboyant in their exorcisms and cures but even "take upon them the name of Christ falsely, and say: We teach the truth, and yet go wandering about idly, and exalt themselves, and make their boast" (1 Epistle 11).

Like the idle widows in First Timothy who are worthless gossips, these men

do not work, but go hunting for tales and think to themselves that this is profitable and right. For such persons are like those idle and prating widows "who go wandering about among houses" with their prating, and hunt for idle tales, and carry them from house to house with much exaggeration, without fear of God. And besides all this, barefaced men as they are, under pretence of teaching, they set forth a variety of doctrines. And would that they taught the doctrines of truth! But it is this which is so disquieting, that they understand not what they mean, and assert that which is not true: because they wish to be teachers, and to display themselves as skillful in speaking; because they traffic in iniquity in the name of Christ—which it is not right for the servants of God to do. And they hearken not to that which the Scripture has said: "Let not many be teachers among you, my brethren, and be not all of you prophets" (1 Epistle 11).

Evidently many of these men have no homes of their own but accept the hospitality of Christian women. This is especially apparent in the Second Epistle where Pseudo-Clement repeatedly hammers on the theme that proper Christian virgin men would never dwell with virgin women, in contrast to the Christian virgin men known to him who do just that.

The figures Pseudo-Clement finds so displeasing display many of the traits of the second-century apostles whose activities we thought to be hyperbolized in the apocryphal Acts. They claim to be teachers but their teachings are not in accord with those of Pseudo-Clement. Homeless itinerants, they go from house to house, wander about idly, and dwell with Christian women. They would, however, have made a powerful impression with their exorcisms and adjurations. Pseudo-Clement states that they read Scripture, teach, exorcise, and cure; he describes their efforts in these regards as flamboyant and impressive. They exalt themselves and speak "terrible words which affright people." They would be remembered and held in considerable awe.

Significantly, Pseudo-Clement says disapprovingly that these men do not work and are idle. Pseudo-Clement himself values work and workmen, using the term "workman" repeatedly as a metaphor for "proper Christian" (1 Epistle 13). There seems no reason to doubt that his church was in acceptable financial shape and able to support dependent women, and that his opponents who did not work could not have done so.

It seems quite possible that the continent Christians behind the Acts and the Epistles dwelt in the same region at the same time and encountered the same kind of itinerant Christian preachers. In the Acts these preachers may have formed the basis for a conception of ideal apostles as men who associated closely with women. In the Epistles the same preachers seem to have been anathematized for their association with women while the first apostles were held up as ideal exemplars of sexual segregation.

Such preachers, whom we have been calling "apostles," seem to have been able to retain the possibility of close association with continent Christian women because they remained in a particular place for only a limited period of time. They travel from town to town in the apocryphal Acts and from home to home in both Pseudo-Clement's Epistles and in the Acts of Xanthippe. Their liaisons might have been both brief and intense.

Visions reported in the Acts indicate that these men were seen to be like Christ by widows and, indeed, Pseudo-Clement reports that they "took upon them the name of Christ" (1 Epistle 11). If they were in some fashion apprehended as being like Christ by "brides of Christ" and if they departed from those "brides" soon after having arrived and established a relationship with them, the women could be in the position of lovers deserted by their beloved. This facet of the apostles' impact might account, to some extent, for the reports in the apocryphal Acts of persons desolated by the fact that an apostle departs.

The Acts show that the relationship between apostles and the women they preached to, exorcised, and taught was intense, mutually respectful, and brief. All parties were determined to maintain sexual continence. Through the itinerance of the apostles sexual relations were rendered unlikely, just as they were by the cold aloofness of continent Christian men like Pseudo-Clement.

The women in such a community would have probably been financially dependent on men like Pseudo-Clement and emotionally drawn to itinerant apostles. One further option appears to have been open to continent Christians of different sexes: the establishment of spiritual marriage between two continent individuals. Pseudo-Clement is unambiguous in his disapproval of such an arrangement; the apocryphal Acts approve it only for married couples who both convert to Christianity. Even in the spiritual marriages mentioned in the Acts the men are often depicted as weak, almost foolish characters (e.g., Probus in Xanthippe, Lycomedes and Andronicus in John). The option of spiritual marriage seems to have been generally regarded as dangerous, subject to overwhelming tension and temptation.

Insofar as the Epistles of Pseudo-Clement on virginity shed light on the way of life and thought of sexually continent second-century Christians, they lend support to the hypothesis that the Acts derive from communities of continent women. The Epistles show that the alternative hypothesis, that the Acts derive from communities of continent Christian men, does not accord with second-century social reality. Virgin men like Pseudo-Clement could not have shown idealized apostles in continuous close contact with women and could not have participated in sexually integrated groups. Further, such men as Pseudo-Clement and his "brethren" could not have written the Acts for the purpose of the edification of women; such men found the sexual integration the Acts depict dangerous and abhorrent. If these men did not write the Acts and if the Acts were not written by such church officials as bishops, presbyters, or deacons (who neither expressed their own concerns in the Acts nor shared in the Acts' absolute dedication to sexual continence), then who did write them?

They were quite possibly written by continent Christian women.

VI

The Authorship of the Acts

THE APOCRYPHAL ACTS seem to have originated from a community made up in great part of continent Christian women. This rather startling conclusion implies a corollary thesis which, at first glance, seems even more startling: that many of the apocryphal Acts were written by women. In this chapter we will argue that this thesis is more probable than a thesis that the Acts were written by men.

The common assumption that men wrote the Acts stems from the principle of Ockham's razor. According to this principle, a theory which requires the least special pleading and complex formulation is (all other things being equal) most probably true. Therefore scholars assume that, because the great bulk of ancient Christian literature of known authorship was written by men, documents of unknown authorship were more probably written by men than by women. However, the principle of Ockham's razor is without value in a situation where evidence exists to support a particular theory. Although female authorship of the apocryphal Acts cannot be proved beyond doubt, it ceases to be a radical and startling idea once one realizes that the contrary position is supported *only* by the notion that, because other documents were written by men, then documents of unknown authorship must also have been written by men.

Given the prejudice of our culture, there is no solace in maintaining that unknown authors are, ipso facto, of indeterminate sex; Ockham's razor will intervene to restore the notion that male authorship must be assumed in the absence of evidence to the contrary. Consider, if you will, that if we were here arguing that the apocryphal Acts were written by the men of the early church no eyebrows would be raised. The argument for female authorship is surprising precisely because it is assumed that all authors of anonymous documents are male.

Our argument for female authorship will follow the classic pattern: opportunity, means, and motive. We will for the most part avoid speculations that a "woman's point of view" prevails in the Acts, because what might count for such a point of view among the continent Christian women of the latter second century cannot be known. We will assume our previous conclusion that the Acts are addressed to an audience which was predominantly female. The Acts' authors, therefore, were persons directly concerned with the edification and entertainment of continent Christian women.

We are faced with the task of determining who might have been most directly concerned with ministering regularly to continent Christian women. Those responsible for this ministry will be leading candidates for the authorship of documents intended to edify Christian women. We have already ruled out both the formal male hierarchy of the church and "virgin" men as likely candidates. Evidence indicates that in the early Church the daily informal ministry to women was carried on by women.

The Shepherd of Hermas from the second century mentions a woman named Grapte whose duty it was to communicate messages to widows just as one Clement was to communicate messages to non-Roman churches. In Grapte we have a woman with a special ministry to women; in the opinion of Stählin, "Grapte in Herm. v., 2,4,3 was probably a deaconess who cared for widows and orphans spiritually as well as physically."[1] "The deaconess," writes Mary Lawrence McKenna, "inherited the missionary role women played in the church from the day of its birth. She was the successor of the women who accompanied the apostles, those whom Paul mentioned in 1. Corinthians 9:5, as she was sent by the bishops to the

---

1. Stählin, "Chēra," p. 461.

women in pagan houses."[2] The deaconess was expected to maintain complete sexual continence. "According to the Apostolic Constitutions, the deaconess had to be either a pure virgin or a widow married only once (VI, 17, 4). The deaconess's 'vow of chastity' is specifically referred to in ecclesiastical legislation. In his Letter 199 St. Basil prescribed in the fourth century that a deaconess who violated her vow of chastity was to undergo the punishment meted out to clerics."[3]

In a lengthy passage McKenna writes of the duties of primitive deaconesses, drawing her evidence from ancient Christian sources:

In the rapidly expanding early church [the deaconess's] task of instructing woman candidates for baptism was no small one. It required of the deaconess a certain level of education.

Those chosen for the ministry of the baptism of women should be so instructed for this office that they can teach uneducated women with apt and sound words how they should answer the baptismal question at the time of their baptism, and how they should live once they are baptized. (*Statuta ecclesiae antiqua, Canon 12*)

But although the deaconess's role in the baptism of women may have been the "first" among her functions, it was evidently not her only one. She was necessary for "many other things" as well, as the Didascalia unfolds.

Therefore, O Bishop, you shall constitute fellow workers of justice, helpers who will help your people toward life. You shall choose those who please you from among all the people and establish them as deacons: men so that they may care for numerous necessary things, *women for the ministry among women*. For there are houses into which you cannot send the deacon to the women because of the gentiles, but you can send the deaconess. And for many other things also the post of women deaconesses is necessary. (III, 12, 1–2; also *Const. apost.* III, 16, 1–2) (emphasis added)

In general the deaconess paralleled among the women the function of the deacon among the men. Both were the helpers of the bishop in the dis-

2. McKenna, *Women of the Church*, p. 71.
3. Ibid., p. 80.

charge of his multiform responsibilities toward the bodies and souls of his
flock: the deacon among the men, the deaconess among the women.[4]

This material demonstrates that some women in the early church
were directly charged with ministry to women, a ministry more
intimate and commonplace than the formal ministry of men to
women. When the Didascalia refers to "houses into which you cannot send the deacon to the women," reference is possibly being
made to women sequestered from contact with all men but their
husbands. The Acts seem to have derived from regions where such
sequestering occurred. In the Acts of Thomas, a husband says to his
newly Christian wife, "Why didst thou not have regard to thy
position as a free woman and remain in thy house?" (A.Th. 9:89)
There is a similar report in the Acts of Peter about Eubula who
comes to court "whereas she had never (before) come out in public" (A.Pt. 6:17). Polyxena, in the Acts of Xanthippe, having been
kidnapped, says, "Woe is me, who at one time showed myself not
even to my servants, and now display myself to demons" (A.Xn.
26). The apocryphal Acts apparently come from regions where
women were at times kept in seclusion; in such regions only other
women, called deaconesses in the Didascalia, might have conve-
niently performed "ministry among women."[5]

Origen writes, in his sixth homily on Isaiah: "And these widows
are worthy to be honored in the Church who wash the feet of the
saints through spiritual instruction—by saints I mean not men but
women. For: 'I permit no woman to teach or to have authority
over men'. He wants women 'to teach what is good', in the sense

4. Ibid., pp. 69–70.

5. Exactly how secluded from life outside the home women were is a disputed
matter. Ryrie writes: "Thus we may conclude that in the Greek world the status of
women was decidedly inferior to that of men; wives led lives of seclusion and practical slavery; the *hetairai*, though enjoying more freedom of movement at least, did
not share the rights or status that belonged to men; and the relative freedom which
did come to women in places like Macedonia was enjoyed only by a minority" (*The
Role of Women in the Church*, p. 5). Leonard Swidler concludes that "the status of
women was quite high in the Hellenistic and Roman worlds into which Christianity
moved. But after the disappearance of those cultures many restrictions on women
appeared in the Christian world" ("Greco-Roman Feminism and the Reception of
the Gospel," in *Traditio-Krisis-Renovatio aus Theologischer Sicht*, ed. B. Jaspert and
R. Mohr, p. 54).

that they have to inculcate chastity in 'young women' not young men, for it is not becoming for a woman to be a teacher of men; but they must train young women in chastity and love of their husbands and children."[6] It is evident that widows, like deaconesses, had the duty of instructing other women in the faith. There appears to have been a general tendency for women to have the duty of teaching and ministering to other women, especially in times and places where men who went to the homes of married women or unmarried daughters would be viewed warily or forbidden entry altogether. The persons with the greatest opportunity to minister regularly and informally to women were other women. And women in need of formal ministry by women were no rarity, widows were numerous. Eusebius (*Historia Ecclesiastica* 6.43.11) writes that the church in Rome had one bishop, forty-six presbyters, seven deacons, seven subdeacons, forty-two acolytes, fifty-two exorcists, readers, and doorkeepers, and more than fifteen hundred widows and persons in distress!

Rosemary Ruether writes, in her essay "Mothers of the Church," that

What individuals find "liberating" is relative, but perhaps the most important common denominator of the liberating choice is the sense of taking charge of one's own life; of rejecting a state of being governed and defined by others. One experiences the sense of moving from being an object to becoming a subject. I would argue that asceticism could be and was experienced as that kind of liberating choice for women in the fourth century, for not only did it allow women to throw off the traditional female roles, but it offered female-directed communities where they could pursue the highest self-development as autonomous persons. It also offered security, for wealthy women endowed these communities for themselves and others. As a result, throngs of women were attracted to asceticism at this time, especially as the old Roman way of life was disintegrating.[7]

This observation was true for isolated communities of women in the fourth century. During the charismatic formative stages of the church, however, women found such self-development possible in

6. Gryson, trans., *The Ministry of Women in the Early Church*, p. 27.
7. Ruether, "Mothers of the Church: Ascetic Women in the Late Patristic Age," in *Women of Spirit*, ed. R. Ruether, p. 73.

the Christian movement rather than only in female-directed communities within that movement. Elisabeth Schüssler Fiorenza describes this era:

New analyses of the social world of early Christianity which show it, not as a culturally well-adapted, monolithic group, but as an egalitarian, countercultural, multifaceted movement suggest an alternate view [to that of women's marginal importance]. This view becomes clear when all the early sources, apocryphal and heterodox as well as canonical and orthodox, are examined. Membership in this egalitarian, pluriform movement was not defined by gender roles, but by faith commitment to the Christian community. Women, in this egalitarian movement, were not marginal figures but exercised responsible leadership.

During the early missionary period, leadership roles were diversified and based on actual function and service. Gradually these became institutionalized and a patriarchalization of the Christian community, offices and theology took place, as the early Christians adopted the institutional forms of the surrounding patriarchal culture. Charismatic leadership rooted in the experience of and in the obedience to the Spirit was gradually replaced by patriarchal office and cultic ministry. This development was not the same in all places, but followed different patterns in various Christian groups. The patriarchal line of early Christian development played down women's role or made it marginal. But the earlier countercultural and later extra-ecclesial groups accepted women as equal members with equal responsibility and leadership.[8]

The apocryphal Acts seem to derive from a transitional period. The church of charismatic leadership wherein women found significant leadership roles was becoming both institutional and patriarchal. As the opportunity for leadership in the whole church diminished for women, female-directed communities came into being. We find in the Acts on the one hand the remnant of a charismatic Christianity wherein women could still play central roles and, on the other hand, the beginning of ascetic communities of women.

Women had ample opportunity to compose written materials for the enjoyment and edification of other women; they were also capable of doing so. For some reason many people find it difficult to

8. Fiorenza, "Word, Spirit and Power: Women in Early Christian Communities," in *Women of Spirit*, ed. R. Ruether, pp. 30–31.

believe that a good number of women in the ancient world were literate. Women could read, and women could write. "And if Hellenistic literature, particularly the novel, was written for a feminine audience, as Erwin Rohde has claimed, then it was without doubt addressed to the women of the educated circles of Alexandria, Athens, and such cities in Asia Minor and Greece."[9] It is certainly true that women of the wealthier classes would be more likely to receive education than poorer women, but the same is true for men. Like men, women in the ancient world might embark on literary careers. "In Rome, both Stoic and Epicurean philosophers encouraged the public education of women and advocated egalitarian women-men relationships. The support of this intellectual elite not only contributed to making change in the legal status of women but also helped make it possible for at least some upper-class women to achieve vocational recognition as poets, writers and historians."[10] Such education was part of the training of middle-class women and the daughters of the wealthier slaves. Ludwig Friedländer writes that:

Daughters in the higher ranks received learned instruction at home; only the smaller people sent their girls every morning to early school, to be disciplined by the master, "so hated both of boys and girls", and both sexes were (perhaps up to a certain age only) instructed together. Martial asks: "is it a poet's ambition to be read out loud by a hoarse and pompous schoolmaster to an unsympathetic crowd of boys and girls?" The tomb of a schoolmaster at Capua depicts an elderly man on a high seat on his right a boy, on his left a girl. . . . The higher instruction of girls is seldom mentioned but seems to have been the same as the boys', reading and explaining poets in both languages. Boys and girls, says Ovid, read Menander, though he is nothing but love-stories.[11]

The literate, educated woman in the ancient world was not an exception in the wealthier classes; she was the ideal. "Quintilian, in his De institutione Oratoria, says, both parents should be as cul-

9. Preaux, "Le statut de la femme à l'époque hellénistique," *Recueil de la Société Jean Bodin* 11, no. 1 (1959):172.

10. Parvey, "The Theology and Leadership of Women in the New Testament," in *Religion and Sexism*, ed. Ruether, p. 118.

11. Friedländer, *Roman Life and Manners*, p. 230.

tured as possible, not only the father. Martial's ideal woman is rich, noble, erudite and chaste. Ovid, who in his Ars Amatoria assures the reader he is speaking only of libertines, but is nevertheless describing women, says: 'There is a small circle of learned women, genuine or specious.' . . . In Augustus' home, which constantly encouraged literature, the women had to embrace it." [12] Examples could be multiplied of noble women who were literate and erudite. Our purpose is not, however, to survey education in the ancient Roman world but simply to remind the reader that in that world literate women were no rarity.

The apocryphal Acts present the adherents of apostles as, by and large, drawn from the very wealthiest classes of society. This characteristic is more probably an instance of the Acts' ubiquitous tendency to hyperbole than the faithful reporting of a reality. On the other hand, since converts to the faith in the Acts are so frequently depicted as wealthy, the community behind the Acts probably knew of the conversion of at least some such women. There is no reason to doubt that many members of the community behind the Acts were from at least the middle classes and thus that many were literate. In the Acts of Xanthippe the woman Xanthippe is shown to be perfectly capable of reading Scripture (A.Xn. 22); her literacy is not taken by the narrator of the Acts to be anything out of the ordinary.

Women had the opportunity to compose edifying and entertaining tales in the course of a female ministry which existed among the sexually continent women of the early Christian church. Furthermore, educated and literate women were not rare in the ancient world. We are left with the problem of motive, of understanding why women might have wished to compose documents like the apocryphal Acts.

We know that it was a duty of highly regarded continent women in the church to educate other women both in the Christian style of life and in Christian doctrine. The apocryphal Acts, when not de-

---

12. Ibid., p. 251; see also Parvey, who believes that "one possible reason for so much emphasis on women in [the canonical] Acts is that the early Church had more success among women, especially in the middle and upper classes" ("The Theology and Leadership of Women," in *Religion and Sexism*, p. 143). Women of those classes would have been, of course, more likely to be literate than women of lower classes.

scribing the exploits of charismatic apostles, contain doctrinal discourses and descriptions of female exemplars of the continent style of Christian life. In this way they are educational and, as discussed above, their edificatory intent is directed toward women. Since it was the duty of women to conduct a regular, informal, teaching ministry to other women in the early church, and since the Acts appear to be edificatory documents intended for a predominantly female audience, the Acts could have been a product of the ministry of women to women.

The Acts are written by persons who had a highly positive view of female Christians and who are interested in communicating that view to others. Such a positive view toward women was, to say the least, uncommon among the Church Fathers known to us from the late second and early third centuries. To quote Rosemary Ruether: "Tertullian demands an abasement of woman and the covering of her shameful female nature as the consequence of her continuing imaging of the guilty nature of Eve. . . . Even the mild Clement of Alexandria, who defends more generously than some of the other Fathers, the spiritual equivalence of woman with man and the dignity of marriage as a relationship, speaks of woman as having to blush for shame 'when you think of what nature you are.'"[13] This sort of denigration is absent from the Acts, which present females as sinful, as capable of positive transformation, and as exemplary. They do not, as does Methodius in the *Symposium*, for instance, set up as models ethereal female figures of unattainable perfection. Women in the Acts are neither benighted creatures forever burdened by the shame of their sex nor are they placed on pedestals of perfection.

We find in the Acts a positive and fairly realistic view of female Christians, which could serve to bolster, not to undermine, the self-image of women in the church. The residue of the kind of anti-female attitude Ruether discovers in patristic literature can be found in the Acts: the responsibility of Eve for the Fall is mentioned in the Acts of Xanthippe, the notion that continent women should adopt the garb of a man occurs in the Acts of Paul. But these instances are only a residue not supported by argument and with no trace of the

13. Ruether, "Virginal Feminism in the Fathers of the Church," in *Religion and Sexism*, ed. R. Ruether, p. 157.

assumption that the female sex is inherently shameful. Sometimes what appear to be antifemale indications can be otherwise explained. For instance, male garb may have functioned for continent women like "habits" and served symbolically to dissuade men from initiating sexual advances. One must remain careful, when reading the Acts, not to confuse their unrelenting opposition to sexual intercourse with opposition to women.

Judging by the early patristic material known to us, we see that many of the leading men of the early church were prone to an attitude of disdain for the female sex. The Acts may well have been an expression of resistance to this stance, an assertion of positive self-valuation on the part of continent Christian women.

The apocryphal Acts perhaps take the form they do because very few other options were open to women in the Christian church for literary self-expression. The prohibition against women teaching men was early, powerful, and almost universal in the church. In the Montanist and Marcionite movements the teaching of men by women was not as strongly discouraged. However, given their almost complete disinterest in prophecy, the Acts cannot be considered Montanist; and they show no trace of the fundamental Marcionite rejection of the world's creator. In the rest of the church women seem to have been prohibited from teaching men. Therefore, women did not have the option of composing theological treatises or moral homilies for general distribution.

The Acts are documents primarily directed to women but also available to the general Christian populace. The teachings they contain would have had to seem to derive from men and not from women for, otherwise, the Acts (if written by women) would have been suppressed by the church hierarchy. Tertullian, for instance, tried to suppress the Acts of Paul for advocating the right of women even to preach to men.[14] The apocryphal Acts were, prima facie, composed by persons who believed they could disseminate their ideas best by attributing them to revered male figures of the past. Attribution of teachings to first-century apostles would reduce the danger that a female author would be persecuted for teaching men and would guarantee a certain respectability to her ideas.

Men, of course, might just as easily as women have put words

14. Tertullian *De Baptismo* 17.

into the mouths of revered apostles, but men had other alternatives: homilies, sermons, epistles, commentaries, antiheretical writings, and apologies. If a woman wished to write for a broader audience than her limited circle of fellow Christian townswomen, she would have few alternatives other than to attribute her ideas to an absent man. This does not, of course, prove female authorship, but it does appear that in those times pseudepigraphical works were among the very few options open to a woman who wished to express herself in writing to a fairly wide Christian audience.

It seems to be the case, however, that the apocryphal Acts are not simply disguised homilies composed by individuals. They seem to have arisen out of the experience of some Christians with itinerant wonder-working Christian preachers whose teachings, we may assume, are reflected in many of the teachings attributed in the Acts to the Christ's apostles. The Acts' teachings are, therefore, most probably a distillation of the ideas of their authors, ideas gleaned from various Christian itinerants, and ideas taught within the formal setting of the church.

Thus far we have tried to avoid the problematic matter of "a woman's point of view" and to show that female authorship of the Acts is a very reasonable hypothesis for a variety of social and contextual reasons. However, if any of the Acts lend themselves to argument focusing on "a woman's point of view" the Acts of Paul do, particularly in the Thecla sequence. In a previous section of this study we have pointed out that Thecla's second round of tortures in the arena is presented as a direct and continuous opposition between males and females: the "women" oppose the "people," the queen opposes the governor, a lioness opposes the other beasts, and other examples discussed in chapter 4. The author of this work shows considerable sensitivity to the problems a woman may have encountered in the attempt to live a Christian life; passionate men, backed up by male-dominated civil authority, seek to use her sexually. Christian men, exemplified by the apostle Paul, do not take her seriously but regard her as a beautiful woman, prone to temptation despite her status as a confessor. The author of this work was someone deeply resentful of the male sex and highly sensitive to the difficulties of women.

In the second torture sequence there is a passage worthy of considerable attention. Thecla had just baptized herself:

There was about her a cloud of fire, so that neither could the beasts touch her nor could she be seen naked. But as other more terrible beasts were let loose, the women cried aloud, and some threw petals, others nard, others cassia, others amomum, so that there was an abundance of perfumes. And all the beasts let loose were overpowered as if by sleep, and did not touch her. So Alexander said to the governor: "I have some very fearsome bulls —let us tie her to them." The governor frowning gave his consent, saying: "Do what thou wilt." And they bound her by the feet between the bulls, and set red-hot irons beneath their bellies that being the more enraged they might kill her. The bulls indeed leaped forward, but the flame that blazed around her burned through the ropes, and she was as if she were not bound (A.Pl. 3:35).

This passage is a graphic portrayal of sexual sadism. A beautiful naked woman with her legs ripped apart by bulls enraged to a frenzy by the application of hot irons to their sexual organs—such an image could only come from a disturbed mind. Thecla is assaulted in this fashion at the urging of Alexander, who instigated her tortures because she resisted his sexual advances; civil authority gives way to his wishes while women (and God) represent his opposition. Men, civil authority, and sexual sadism stand here in juxtaposition to God and women.

The author of the Acts of Paul was either a woman or a man. If the author was a man, his imagery of sexual torture renders almost incomprehensible his awareness of and sensitivity to the difficulties of Christian women in their relations with Christian men. Sympathetic sensitivity to the difficulties of women and wildly sadistic descriptions of the torture of women can only with great difficulty be thought to have been attitudes held by the same man. A male author's sensitivity to the problems of women would have to stem from sympathy; a female author's sensitivity would stem from experience. If the author was female she would still be somewhat disturbed, but her attitudes would take on a certain consistency. Her distaste for the slights of men and their sexual intentions might, when exaggerated, lead her to depict the inimical behavior of men in the most graphic terms possible, e.g., as bulls enraged by their burning phalluses. The hypothesis of female authorship eliminates the contradiction between sympathetic sensitivity and sadistic imagery and replaces it with a simple contrast between greater and lesser expressions of resentment. As we can see from the Life of St. Syncletica, wherein parallels are drawn with Thecla's life, and from a commentary by Gregory of Nyssa that his sister Macrina resembled "Thecla, . . . *so famous among the virgins*" (emphasis added), the Thecla story found great favor among the continent women of the early church.[15]

Male authorship of the Acts of Paul, and in particular the Thecla sequence, requires an author who has an almost pathologically negative sexual self-image, an author who combines sympathy with sadistic imaginings. Female authorship of that document requires an author with a positive sexual self-image and a wide range of resentment against men. The latter hypothesis is by far the simpler and requires fewer assumptions. It might be possible to compose a psychological profile of a man who might have written the document, but it would be a difficult task. Female authorship, seemingly a radical notion, is actually much easier to defend.[16]

15. Nugent, *Portrait of the Consecrated Woman in Greek Christian Literature of the First Four Centuries*, p. 82.

16. See also Alice Gardener's comments on the apocryphal Acts:

The stories of women who broke away from the ties of betrothal or even of marriage in order to share in the lives and labours of the Apostles are, of course, of doubtful historical value. It has been pointed out that in some cases the story fits in so well with known historical surroundings as to give it a certain amount of probability; also that, even if untrustworthy as to facts, it may be important as giving indications both of life and manners and of institutions. . . . Yet, though the relations of Paul to Thekla and of Philip to Mariamne may be set down to fancy pure and simple, they are at least evidence of an atmosphere that may have helped to develop some ambitions of a peculiar kind in emotional women of the sub-Apostolic period (in Report of the Archbishop of Canterbury's Committee on the Ministry of Women, *The Ministry of Women*, app. 5, p. 80).

We agree with Gardener with the single exception that we believe the apocryphal Acts developed *from* the ambitions of certain women. These ambitions may have even been, in the context of their time, revolutionary: Parvey observes that "for women, celibacy was revolutionary," legitimatizing "an independent vocational status. They could choose not to raise families and have husbands. They could choose from a variety of leadership positions within the Christian community and yet remain celibate." Moreover, celibacy had never been "an option of Jewish women," and Roman laws "prohibited women from remaining single and made it mandatory for them to remarry after divorce or widowhood. It was only through Christianity that celibacy for women became a socially acceptable status for them" ("The Theology and Leadership of Women," in *Religion and Sexism*, pp. 135, 149 n. 34). The social acceptability of this status was only intra-Christian. Both virgins who would not marry and widows who would not remarry broke Roman law.

Tertullian mentions the Acts of Paul in the course of a diatribe against women who claim rights he believes should be reserved for men.

The impudence of that woman who assumed the right to teach is evidently not going to arrogate to her the right to baptize as well—unless perhaps some new serpent appears, like that original one, so that as the woman abolished baptism, some other should of her own authority confer it. But if certain Acts of Paul which are falsely so named, claim the example of Thecla for allowing women to teach and to baptize, let men know that in Asia the [*presbites*] who compiled that document, thinking to add of his own to Paul's reputation, was found out, and though he professed he had done it for love of Paul, was deposed from his position. How could we believe that Paul should give a female power to teach and to baptize, when he did not allow a woman even to learn by her own right?[17]

There is, however, no reason to assume that Tertullian was very well informed about the affairs of individual churches in Asia, especially since the document he happily reports to have been condemned with the resultant humiliation of its author seems to have enjoyed great favor in the eastern churches after this time. Tertullian is notorious for his willingness to manipulate fact in the interest of rhetorical flourish. Further, the Acts of Paul in the Thecla sequence (against which Tertullian is arguing) does little to add to Paul's reputation although Tertullian says that this was their supposed purpose. Unfortunately, the report in Tertullian about the Acts of Paul seems to be too ambiguous and unreliable to be used as evidence for or against the position that a woman was the author of those Acts.

We can conclude, from these and other considerations, that Ockham's razor ought henceforth to cut the other way—that female authorship of the apocryphal Acts ought to be assumed in the absence of any convincing argument to the contrary. Were the Acts authored by men they would be men without high official position in the church, devoted to the life-style of sexual chastity but eager to associate with women, determined to promulgate a positive view

17. Gryson, trans., *Ministry of Women*, p. 18; for the reading *presbites* rather than *presbyterum* (as one would expect) cf. A. Souter, "The 'Acta Pauli' etc. in Tertullian," *Journal of Theological Studies* 25(1924):292.

of the female sex and to create models of exemplary women, greatly concerned with the financial well-being of widows and virgins of the Lord, devoted to wandering charismatic apostles, willing to hide their own identities while putting words in the mouths of apostles of the first century, and prone to adopt the ancient love romance as the model for their own literary efforts. If anyone can bring evidence for the existence of men of this sort and argue that they, and not literate widows or deaconesses, composed the Acts, then the hypothesis of female authorship will be refuted. Until that time Christian women should be given credit for the creativity which remains embodied in their compositions, the apocryphal Acts of the Apostles.

VII

Conclusion

A HISTORICAL CASE must always be made through argument and reasoned speculation, concluding only with a claim for probability and not for certainty. The preceding portion of this study has been such a case, and so concludes. But we are not constrained to stop thinking altogether. We can speculate quite a bit more about the way of life of the Christian women who probably wrote the apocryphal Acts.

The women featured in the Acts are never Christians born into the church; all are converted. Often married or betrothed, they must choose between family and church, between husband and Christ, between their old and their new bridegroom. The Acts do not condemn marriage per se, but they do condemn the sexual intercourse entailed by marriage; and they encourage women to assert themselves to refuse to submit to the desires of their husbands. If their husbands object, and refuse to allow their wives to live continently, then the flight of women from home and spouse is urged.

Rosemary Ruether, in her essay "Misogynism and Virginal Feminism in the Fathers of the Church," shows that such rebellion is contrary to the teachings of the Church Fathers, who believed that married women should submit without complaint to the role of wife. "As wife, woman is also essentially body, but now the image of that totally submissive body, obedient to her 'head' which serves the male without a murmur even under harsh and unjust treatment. Such a woman has no personal rights over her own body, but must surrender her body to her husband on command, receiving from such use no personal pleasure, but allowing herself to be used solely as an instrument of procreation."[1] This passage, which is Ruether's summation of the attitudes held by the Church Fathers, is in stark contrast to the rebelliousness urged in the Acts. Women there are urged to command their own bodies and to resist their husbands in the pursuit of Christian perfection.

Married men had on their side the force of civil authority determined to protect the institution of marriage and to enforce the Roman laws which required maximum reproduction. A woman determined to free herself from a husband's authority would have had to equate closely two virtues: endurance and chastity. The virtue of endurance in such a situation becomes tantamount to denying the legitimacy of civil authority. Action which accompanies such denial is rebellion.

Patristic literature shows that a majority of the men who were church leaders thought there was no difficulty in being both Christian and married. In the Acts, apostles do not materially assist women in breaking away from their marriages. This the women do alone. Apostles provide only the initial impetus and later moral support. Even their moral support occasionally flags. Thomas, fearful of the anger of Mygdonia's spurned husband, urges Mygdonia to return to him. When Thecla is tortured for refusing marriage to her fiancé, Paul vanishes from the scene. In the Acts of Xanthippe Paul seemingly encourages Probus in his desire to have his wife, Xanthippe, resume marital relations with him: "The great Paul was teaching thus, 'Let those that burn in the flesh observe lawful marriage, avoiding fornication, especially that with another's wife, and let those that are united keep to one another.' Probus heard this teaching with delight, and said, 'O Paul, how excellently and wisely thou employest this teaching. Why then has Xanthippe withdrawn from me?'" (A.Xn. 20) The Acts show us no male heroes successfully aiding women to escape their hus-

1. Ruether, "Virginal Feminism," p. 164.

bands' control; the widows face the challenge alone or with other women (for example, Maximilla with Iphidamia, Xanthippe with Polyxena, Mygdonia with Tertia).

If we take seriously the Acts' assumption that sexual continence is essential to the perfect Christian life, the difficulties of Christian women who are married, especially those married to non-Christian men (a not uncommon circumstance in the years 160–225) can be seen to have been immense. Women were urged by the male church hierarchy to remain submissive and remain married; yet simultaneously men preached a vision of perfection *open to women*, which women were denied by virtue of marital intercourse. Only in continence might a woman become spiritually equal to men, and only to the continent could come the full benefit of the Christian faith. Ruether, writing of the age of Augustine, says: "In this twilight period of antiquity, we see, then, the image of the virginal woman appearing as a new cultural ideal, raising up the possibility of woman as capable of the highest spiritual development, which could lead to the *summum bonum* of communion with the divine, intellectual nature of the Divine itself."[2] In the Acts of Andrew Maximilla is praised in the language of Christian gnosticism as one who has shared in this goal. She is "immaterial, holy, light, akin to him that is unbegotten, . . . intellectual, heavenly, translucent, pure," etc. (A.An. Cod. Vat. 6) In the time of persecutions, when Christianity was far from an accepted religious option, a married or betrothed woman who was converted would have wished for more than the half-measure of Christian potential allotted to the incontinent wife. Her options would have been, however, to accept that half measure, to wait patiently for her husband's death in hopes of achieving widowhood (surely an unpalatable option), or to choose the path of rebellion, fly in the face of social norms and the preaching of Christian men and seek the *summum bonum* offered as reward for the continent life.

Whether a marriage might or might not be broken up or a betrothal ended if a man demanded his wife's sexual submission is not simply a matter separating sects. It is a matter separating men who encouraged the submission of wives and women who encouraged wives to strive after what they took to be the highest good. Many

2. Ibid., p. 178.

Christian women, judging by the apocryphal Acts, seem to have found the prospects of freedom opened by Christianity to include the option of freedom to escape from marital intercourse and (if necessary) marriage itself. The Acts, then, are evidence of a rebellion within the Christian church as well as a rebellion of women against their husbands. In both cases general norms are set aside in the desire of women to rise to the heights possible to Christians.

The freedom to escape from marital intercourse asserted in all apocryphal Acts is radical both in terms of the ancient social order and in terms of the Christian male church order. Rosemary Ruether correctly points out that misogynism and respect for virgin women are not necessarily exclusive categories but in some cases can be two sides of the same coin:

The Church Fathers can simultaneously laud virginity as a liberation from sin, and yet, where women are concerned, prevent that from in any way being interpreted as a liberation for a boldness, integrity, or independence unfitting the "nature of a woman." This evidently came up as a very real pastoral problem in the fourth century, when many women were taking literally the Church's ascetic preaching as a mandate for woman's liberation. Thus, for example, we find Augustine writing to a certain self-willed African matron, Ecducia, who had exacted a vow of continence from her husband and had begun to act with that liberty to dispose of her person and property autonomously befitting one whom the converted life had restored to equivalency with the male! Augustine begins the letter by defining the essential subjugation of woman to man as natural law, and decreeing that the woman has no right to dispose of her own body without male permission: "It is a sin to refuse the debt of your body to your husband."[3]

In advocating the dissolution of marriage and establishing, time and time again, exemplary models of women who have separated from their husbands, the apocryphal Acts do urge liberation. When Xanthippe smashes an astonished demon in the face, when Polyxena and Rebecca brave the dangers in the hills after their rejection by Andrew, when Thecla baptizes herself after having struck Alexander the Syriarch and torn his cloak and stripped the wreath from his head and made him a laughingstock, when Maximilla and

3. Ibid., pp. 159–60.

Drusiana and the myriads of women featured at the conclusion of Peter's Acts fight their way free from marriage or concubinage, the notion of the continent Christian woman as a humble subservient creature disappears.

Having broken free from legal and social bondage to marriage, widows would not have wanted to place themselves in a position of complete and unquestioning subservience to the male church hierarchy. Those not independently wealthy (and they must have been the majority) would have been in an unpleasant situation indeed. Having renounced their husbands, they had, nevertheless, to turn to the established church for financial support. Their renunciation of wealth and fine clothing and their desire for simple foods and fasting would serve to diminish their need for money; but the need would remain. Perhaps the Acts' creation of ideal women as wealthy women derived from the fact that only such women could be truly independent.

Many widows might have found themselves in a position of tension; in becoming Christian they had rebelled against their larger society but, having rebelled, they were given little option but to become again subservient to the male hierarchy of the church, to such men as the author of First Timothy who believed it to be his duty to lay down regulations for widows and dependent women.

The Acts urge rebellion against husbands, and they nowhere encourage complete subservience to the authority of bishops, presbyters, and deacons. They refer back in time to the universally recognized authority of the first-century apostles in whose mouths is put the call to rebellion, the call to Christian continence even if this entails the dissolution of marriages.

As the reader has noticed we are, in this essay, greatly indebted to Rosemary Ruether's observations on the misogynism of the early Church Fathers. She does not here suggest, however, that Christian women might have protested that misogynous attitude. The Acts show that they did protest. The notion that Eve was responsible for the Fall, which Ruether shows to have been held by some Church Fathers, is accepted in the Acts of Andrew, but there it makes the relationship between the Christian woman and Christ (the new Adam) of fundamental importance. She becomes the counterpart to Eve, and it is her return which is crucial to the divine plan. At the conclusion of the Acts of Andrew that apostle seems to

have become a "type" of the new Adam. Andrew says to Maximilla: "I rightly see in you Eve repenting and in myself Adam
being converted: for what she suffered in ignorance you are now
bringing to a happy conclusion because you are converted: and
what the mind suffered which was brought down with her and was
estranged from itself, I put right with you who know that you
yourself are being drawn up. For you yourself who did not suffer
the same things have healed her affliction; and I by taking refuge
with God have perfected his (Adam's) imperfection: and where she
disobeyed, you have been obedient; and where he acquiesced, there
I flee; and where they were made to sin, there we have known. For
it is ordained that everyone should correct his own fall" (A.An.
Cod. Vat. 5). Further, Andrew says: "As Adam died in Eve because
of the harmony of their relationship, so even now I live in you who
keep the command of the Lord and who give yourself over to the
state (dignity) of your (true) Being" (A.An. Cod. Vat. 7). Andrew
concludes by speaking (as Christ/Adam) to Maximilla: "I beg you,
then, the wise man [*sic*[, that your noble mind continue steadfast; I
beg you, the invisible mind, that you may be preserved yourself;
I exhort you, love Jesus and do not submit to the worse; help
me, you, on whose aid as man I call, that I may be perfect; help me,
that you may know your own true nature; suffer with my suffering,
that you may know what I suffer and you will escape suffering"
(A.An. Cod. Vat. 9). Here, we find the dignity of the woman restored by her adherence to the faith. She (as Eve) and Andrew (as
Christ/Adam) together restore the condition of man before the Fall,
a condition of primordial unity such that sexual distinctions vanish
and Maximilla is called "man." This does not imply any denigration of Maximilla or of women in general; women are partners
with men in the work of salvation. Yes, the fault of Eve in the Fall
is stressed, but so is the capacity of women to correct that fault, and
in that capacity women are glorified.

In the Acts of Xanthippe, in a prayer Xanthippe says: "Thou
who didst come from the heart of the father to the heart of the earth
for our sake, on whom the cherubim dare not fix their gaze, and for
us wast hidden in the womb that by taking up thy abode in a
mother thou mightest make good of the offense of Eve. Thou that
didst drink gall and vinegar, and wast pierced in the side by a spear,
that thou mightest heal the wound given by the rib to Adam. For

Eve being his rib wrought a blow for Adam and through him for all the world" (A.Xn. 12). Eve here has become a focal point of the whole myth and Adam a less significant character in the drama of Eve, Christ, Mary, and humanity. This passage is no more indicative of an antifemale attitude than is "in Adam's fall we fell all" an attitude of hostility to males. It is, rather, a shift of emphasis toward Eve which encourages the self-identification of women with Eve such that the perfected Christian woman's life becomes Eve's return.

As some misogyny is present in many writings of the Church Fathers, so some misanthropy is present in the apocryphal Acts. In Ruether's judgment, the writings of the Church Fathers show that "woman is not really seen as a self-sufficient, whole person with equal honor, as the image of God in her own right, but is seen, ethically, as dangerous to the male."[4] In the Acts, on the other hand, men are often seen, ethically, as dangerous to the female. Of course apostles, itinerant charismatic Christian preachers, were highly respected; but such men by the beginning of the third century were a vanishing breed. Men of charismatic works gave way to men of words. The Acts frequently show ordinary Christian men as foolish, confused about the faith, and liable to temptation.

The contempt for men occasionally evident in the Acts may have stemmed from the fact that they were not required, as many widows were, to assert their independence in becoming Christian. Some, like Drusiana's husband Andronicus and Xanthippe's husband Probus, may have become Christians after losing a struggle with their wives; others may have been like the men we know from the Pseudo-Clementine Epistles on Virginity, afraid to touch a female Christian without wrapping their hand in cloth. Ruether finds Jerome to be equally reluctant to touch women, "As Jerome with his strict logic would put it, 'If it is not good to touch a woman, then it is bad to touch a woman' always and in every case."[5] There is an element of simple cowardice in such horror and fear of physical contact. To the widows in the Acts the Christian faith was a rebellious path to religious experience. To the men of the Pseudo-Clementine Epistles it seems to have been a matter of coupling the fear of God with fear of women.

4. Ibid., p. 157.
5. Ibid., p. 166.

Having rejected sexual relations with men, the women behind the Acts seem to have found few men in their Christian communities worthy of substantial respect. They had fled from and rebelled against pagan lovers and husbands, and they had, apparently, little respect for many of the ordinary Christian men who associated with them. Perhaps the women behind the Acts found both an exemplar of masculine perfection and an object of religious reverence in the visionary experience of an immaterial bridegroom. Without delving too far into theological niceties we can know something of the nature of the widows' religious experience and how it forms a consistent pattern with other themes in the Acts. The community behind the Acts commonly experienced visions of Christ. The form in which he appears is always male but otherwise is polymorphous. Christ was seen as a young man, as an old man, as an apostle, as a glorious golden youth.

In the words of Schneemelcher, "encratite ethics and docetic christology often go together"; the denial of the body inherent in a continent life-style and the denial that Christ had a tangible body are closely related.[6] Insofar as the Acts are docetic, this christological stance may have arisen from both visionary experience and dedication to an ascetic continent life-style.

Ruether writes about the relationship between visionary experience and sexual continence:

Modern Freudian psychology can well explain why such a mechanism of repression was bound to be self-defeating, and always to produce its own opposite in obsession with sexual fantasies. Unable to contain this result, asceticism dealt with it in two ways: first, by a pruriency that exercised a perverted sexual libido through constant excoriations of sensuality in ascetic literature; second, by a sublimation of sexual libido that rejected it on the level of physical experience, but allowed it to flourish on the level of fantasy elevated to represent the ecstatic nuptials of the bridal soul with Christ.[7]

[Mary, the] virginal woman was thus bound for heaven, and her male ascetic devotees would stop at nothing short of this prize for her. But they paid the price of despising all real physical women, sex and fecundity, and

---

6. Schneemelcher and Hennecke, eds., *New Testament Apocrypha*, vol. 2, p. 275.
7. Ruether, "Virginal Feminism," p. 167.

wholly etherealizing women into incorporeal phantasms in order to provide love objects for the sublimated libido and guard against turning back
to any physical expression of love with the dangerous daughters of Eve.[8]

In the apocryphal Acts, which are examples of ascetic literature and
are replete with excoriations of sensuality, overtly sexual visionary
experiences are not reported. However, while the men of whom
Ruether writes fantasized Christ's relations with an imaginary
"bridal soul" and imagined an exalted Virgin Mary along with
ethereal incorporeal women, the women in the Acts envisioned
themselves in the presence of their own bridegroom, Christ. Further, they brought forth men in imagination, men with overwhelming divine powers whom they called apostles. Some widows
created apostles, in much the same fashion as some continent
Christian ascetic men created an exalted Virgin Mary, as objects
"for the sublimated libido." If these concepts did not lead to "despising" men, they did go hand in hand with an attitude of some
contempt for men in general (cf. the Thecla sequence of the Acts of
Paul).

Mary Douglas, writing in *Natural Symbols*, informs us that a
group which seeks to seal itself off from external incursion will tend
to symbolize the desire for absolute community isolation through
the strict control of sexual and dining behavior.[9] In other words, a
group determined to form a tight "island" community in the sea of
a larger society will often tend strictly to regulate the exercise of
bodily functions, a tendency which has been called "Encratism."
The extent of the widows' asceticism probably matched the extent
of their alienation from the mainstream of society.

We have seen that sexual continence is related to the bride-
bridegroom metaphor and to the love romance format of the Acts.
Douglas helps us see that continence is also related to the social emphasis on establishing an insular Christian community within but
opposed to the larger society. This emphasis would almost inevita-
bly lead to witchcraft or sorcery accusations against members of the
insular alienated group. Despite such difficulties, in rebellion
against their former husbands, against church leaders who insisted

8. Ibid., p. 179.
9. Douglas, *Natural Symbols*, pp. 93–112.

on the indissolubility of the marital bond while supporting husbands' rights to intercourse, against the fabric of ancient society, the women of the apocryphal Acts sought the *summum bonum* of their Christian faith.

In their reflection on the nature of the Divine these Christian women seem to have retained from speculative gnostic Judaism the notion that there was associated with God a wisdom, or creative power, or spirit which was feminine. This is especially evident in the Acts of Thomas, one of the very earliest known Christian documents from the region of Syria. In an invocation accompanying baptismal anointing, Thomas says:

> Come, holy name of Christ that is above every name;
> Come, power of the Most High and perfect compassion;
> Come, thou highest gift;
> Come, compassionate mother;
> Come, fellowship of the male;
> Come, thou (fem.) that dost reveal the hidden mysteries;
> Come, mother of the seven houses, that thy rest may be in the eighth house (A.Th. 2:27)

Concluding a prayer, the apostle's words are: "we glorify and praise thee and thine invisible Father and thy Holy Spirit and the Mother of all creation" (A.Th. 4:39). In an invocation prior to the Eucharist Thomas says:

> Come, silence
> That dost reveal the great deeds of the whole greatness;
> Come, thou that dost show forth the hidden things
> And make the ineffable manifest;
> Holy Dove
> That bearest the twin young;
> Come, hidden Mother;
> Come, thou that art manifest in thy deeds and dost furnish joy
> And rest for all that are joined with thee;
> Come and partake with us in this Eucharist
> Which we celebrate in thy name,
> And in the love-feast
> In which we are gathered together at thy call. (A.Th. 5:50)

We cannot take these many separate invocations to be requests for the attendance of a plethora of divine beings. Rather we find here in the Acts of Thomas the conception of the Divine as having many aspects, the feminine not least of them. This remarkable willingness to presume that the Divine has feminine aspects is not unique to the Acts of Thomas. In the Acts of Peter there is a prayer wherein Peter says, "Thou art my Father, thou art my Mother, thou my Brother, thou art Friend, thou art Servant, thou art House-keeper, thou art the All, and the All is in thee; thou art Being, and there is nothing that is, except thou" (A.Pt. 9:39). The mystical sensitivity reflected in this prayer appears also in hymns in the Acts of Thomas and the Acts of John. But in those hymns appears not only the notion that God is All, but also the concept of the Divine as Cosmic Dancer. The hymn in the Acts of Thomas is so marvelous that it deserves to be quoted in full:

> The maiden is the daughter of light,
> Upon her stands and rests the majestic effulgence of kings,
> Delightful is the sight of her,
> Radiant with shining beauty.
> Her garments are like spring flowers,
> And a scent of sweet fragrance is diffused from them.
> In the crown of her head the king is established,
> Feeding with his own ambrosia those who are set (under) him.
> Truth rests upon her head,
> By (the movement of) her feet she shows forth joy.
> Her mouth is open, and that becomingly,
> (For with it she sings songs of praise.)
> Thirty and two are they that sing her praises.
> Her tongue is like the curtain of the door,
> Which is flung back for those who enter in.
> (Like steps her neck mounts up,)
> Which the first craftsman wrought.
> Her two hands make signs and secret patterns, proclaiming the dance
>   of the blessed aeons.
> Her fingers (open) the gates of the city.
> Her chamber is full of light,
> Breathing a scent of balsam and all sweet herbs,
> And giving out a sweet smell of myrrh and (aromatic) leaves.

Within are strewn myrtle branches and (all manner of sweet-smelling flowers),
And the (portals) are adorned with reeds.
Her (groomsmen) keep her compassed about, whose number is seven,
Whom she herself has chosen;
And her bridesmaids are seven,
Who dance before her.
Twelve are they in number who serve before her
And are subject to her,
Having their gaze and look toward the bridegroom,
That by the sight of him they may be enlightened;
And for ever shall they be with him in that eternal joy,
    And they shall be at that marriage
For which the princes assemble together,
And shall linger over the feasting
Of which the eternal ones are accounted worthy,
And they shall put on royal robes
And be arrayed in splendid raiment,
And both shall be in joy and exultation
And they shall glorify the Father of All,
Whose proud light they received
And were enlightened by the vision of their Lord,
Whose ambrosial food they received,
Which has no deficiency at all,
And they drank too of his wine
Which gives them neither thirst nor desire;
And they glorified and praised, with the living Spirit,
The Father of Truth and the Mother of Wisdom (A.Th. 1:6–7).

The Acts of Thomas reports that only one person, a young female flute player, understood this hymn when Thomas delivered it. The "daughter of light" with her retinue of seven bridesmaids and groomsmen (corresponding to the seven celestial bodies) and with the twelve who serve before her (the twelve constellations) may be the same as the "Mother of the seven houses," who in an invocation quoted above was asked to accompany, or appear as an aspect of, "the holy name of Christ" and the "power of the Most High." The "daughter of light" is also a Cosmic Dancer, for "by (the movement of) her feet she shows forth joy"; and "her two hands make signs and secret patterns, proclaiming the dance of the blessed aeons." The enlightening vision of the Lord is granted to the widows in the Acts of Peter.

A Cosmic Dancer also appears in the Acts of John. There we find the lovely ritual sometimes known as the "Round Dance" wherein a Cosmic Dancer appears:

> Grace dances.
> I will pipe,   Dance all of you.   Amen
> I will mourn,   Beat you all your breasts.   Amen
> (The) one Ogdoad [Eight] sings praises with us.   Amen
> The twelfth number dances on high.   Amen
> To the Universe belongs the dancer.   Amen
> He who does not dance does not know what happens.   Amen
>   (A.Jn. 94–96).

Compare these lines with A.Th. 2:27, "Come, mother of the seven houses, that thy rest may be in the eighth house." Later in the Round Dance we find these phrases:

> Now if you follow my dance,
> See yourself in Me who am speaking,
> And when you have seen what I do
>   keep silence about my mysteries.
> You who dance, consider what I do, for yours
>   is this passion of Man which I am to suffer.

In the Acts of Andrew, quoted above (A.An. Cod. Vat. 9), we saw that Andrew, speaking as Christ/Adam, identifies himself with Maximilla/Eve in a primordial unity. He says to her, "help me, that you may know your own true nature; suffer with my suffering, that you may know what I suffer and you will escape suffering." It seems reasonable to speculate that the Cosmic Dancer figure is a primordial unity beyond sexual differentiation, one capable of being conceived as "Jesus" or as the "daughter of light" from different perspectives. Perhaps the women in the community behind the apocryphal Acts envisioned final union with their cosmic bridegroom to elevate them to union with the "daughter of light" such that they and their bridegroom together might dance. Seen in this perspective, both the hymn in the Acts of Thomas and the Round Dance in the Acts of John might have formed part of a mystical Cosmic Dancer liturgy practiced by continent Christian women. The ideas of a Cosmic Dancer, of the "daughter of light," of the feminine aspect of God give us intriguing glimpses of a kind of rhythmic Christianity dead now. But among the continent women of the early church these ideas seem to have arisen despite the early orthodox insistence on the masculine nature of the Divine.

The style of thought called gnostic had room for the notion of Divine femininity and the "Round Dance," at least, is often considered gnostic. Ideas contained in that poem occur elsewhere in Christian literature. In his essay "Jesus' Round Dance and Crucifixion according to the Acts of St. John" Max Pulver quotes the poem "Der Minne Weg," by the woman mystic Mechthild of Magdeburgh:

> I would not dance, Lord, unless thou leadest me.
> Wouldst thou that I spring mightily,
> Then must thou sing for me.
> Thus will I leap into love,
> From love into knowledge,
> From knowledge into joy,
> From joy beyond all human senses. . . .[10]

Pulver finds the passage in the "Round Dance," "A mirror am I to thee who discernest me," reminiscent of the Acts of Andrew's phrasing: "Therefore I hold those blessed who have heard the prophecies through which as in a glass they behold the secrets of their own nature, for whose sake all things were created."[11] It is interesting to compare the observations of Pulver on the "Round Dance" with a passage in the Acts of Xanthippe (with which Pulver seems not to be familiar). Pulver writes that John is shown "the implanted cross of light and the formless throng around it. The sole form is in the luminous cross itself. The initiates have entered into the godhead, fused with it. And the mystery god has no longer any

---

10. Pulver, "Jesus' Round Dance and Crucifixion According to the Acts of St. John," in *The Mysteries: Papers from the Eranos Yearbooks*, p. 176.
11. Ibid., p. 190.

outward form but only a voice. His "own," his faithful, that is, make up his form: he is their voice.[12] Xanthippe says, in her Acts, "I desire to keep silence, and am compelled to speak, for some one inflames and sweetens me within. If I say, I will shut my mouth, there is some one that murmurs in me. Shall I say a great thing? Is it not that teacher that is in Paul, without arrogance, filling the heavens, speaking within and waiting without, sitting on the throne with the father and stretched on the cross by man?" (A.Xn. 14)

Irenaeus writes that itinerant gnostic Christian teachers attracted many (and mostly) women.[13] Epiphanius reports, in a revealing passage, that he has had contact with gnostic Christian women:

I have had a brush with this [gnostic] sect myself, beloved, and got my information about its customs in person, straight from the mouths of its members. Women who believed this nonsense offered it to me, and told me the kind of thing I have been describing. In their brazen impudence, what is more, they tried to seduce me. . . . For the women who told me about this salacious myth were outwardly very charming, but all the devil's ugliness was in their vile minds. However, the merciful God saved me from their depravity. . . . And I promptly reported these people to the local bishops, and found which of them were masquerading as members of the church. And so they were driven out of the city, about eighty of them, and it was cleansed of their rank thorny growth.[14]

It is interesting that except for Epiphanius these women would have remained within the church. His accusation has the same ring to it as witchcraft accusations from later periods of Christian history.

Pheme Perkins, writing on the gnostic conception of the apostle Peter, observes that "one line of tradition shows Peter hostile to Mary, who possesses a Gnosis superior to that of the apostle."

The most detailed treatment of this conflict occurs in the Gospel of Mary. Mary shows her superiority to the apostles at the outset. She is the one to encourage the disciples, when they are afraid to undertake the mission of preaching given to them by the risen Lord. Peter, then, asks her to

12. Ibid., p. 192.
13. Irenaeus *Adversus Haereses* 1.6.
14. Robinson, ed., *The Nag Hammadi Library*, p. 5.

share with them a vision she had had of the Savior. But after she is finished, Andrew and Peter raise objections to her account.

The concluding logion of the Gospel of Thomas [number 114] represents another version of this conflict. Peter attempts to have Mary sent away as unworthy of life, but he is overruled by Jesus, who promises to make her male so that she will be eligible to enter the kingdom. Our final witness to the tradition of conflict between Peter and Mary is Pistis Sophia. There, Mary is the major character in questioning Jesus and giving interpretations.[15]

Both "orthodox" and gnostic Christian sources seem to indicate that women found the more gnostic style of Christianity to be particularly in accord with their interests, beliefs, and concerns. We should not be surprised, therefore, that the apocryphal Acts occasionally display gnostic Christian tendencies. The gnostic form of Christianity seems to have been able to advocate the equality of men and women much more effectively than the orthodox form could.[16] Nevertheless, while some of the Acts are touched by gnostic Christian ideas, they are much less so than the recently discovered Nag Hammadi documents.

The apocryphal Acts are an interface between "orthodoxy" and the visionary psycho-cosmogenies of most Nag Hammadi texts.

15. Perkins, "Peter in Gnostic Revelation," *S. B. L. Seminar Papers 1974*.

16. Alice Gardener writes that the church's "tendency towards the restriction of women's powers" might well have led to "an inclination on the part of the restricted to deviate from the beaten track, and at the same time . . . to suspicions of heresy in orthodox but aspiring women" (in Report of the Archbishop of Canterbury's Committee on the Ministry of Women, *The Ministry of Women*, app. 5). Moreover, Ryrie writes, with considerable disapproval, that

In the heterodox sects of the second century, the role of women was important. For evidence of this role, one can consider the place occupied by women of the Gospel in Gnostic literature: Mary, the mother of Jesus, Mary Magdalene, Martha, Salome, etc. . . . The Naassenes pretended that they had received their doctrines from a certain Marianne, who, they said, received them from James, the brother of the Lord. The Acts of Philip introduce Marianne as the sister of this Apostle and associate her with his apostolate, just as the Acts of Paul associate Thecla with the ministry of the Apostle of the Gentiles. (*The Role of Women in the Church*, p. 15)

Finally, the "Dialogue of the Savior" in the Nag Hammadi Codex features, in addition to other disciples, Miriam, who "spoke as a woman who knew the All."

What we have called the "Cosmic Dancer" liturgy is echoed in a few of the Nag Hammadi documents. In the text called "On the Origin of the World" (N.H.C. II,5) there is imagery like that found in the "daughter of light" sequence of the Acts of Thomas. The repentant deity Sabaoth is seated with "Jesus the Christ, who is like the Savior who is above the eighth, sitting at his right upon an excellent throne. But on his left the virgin of the holy spirit sits upon a throne praising him. And the seven virgins stand before her while thirty (other virgins) [with] lyres and harps [and] trumpets in their hands glorify him (II, 5, 105)." [17] The same text also reports an "Eve of Life" who is "the first virgin, not having a husband. When she gave birth, she is the one who healed herself. [Is this Mary?] On account of this it is said concerning her that she said, 'I am the portion of my mother and I am the mother. I am the woman, and I am the virgin. I am the pregnant one and I am the physician. I am the midwife. My husband is the one who begot me, and I am his mother and he is my father and my lord.'" (II, 5.114) This passage is very similar to a passage in "The Thunder, Perfect Mind" (N.H.C. VI, 2) which reads, "I am the wife and the virgin, I am (the mother) and the daughter. I am the members of my mother. I am the barren one and many are her sons. I am she whose wedding is great, and I have not taken a husband. I am the solace of my labor pains. I am the bride and the bridegroom, and it is my husband who begot me. I am the mother of my father and the sister of my husband, and he is my offspring." (VI, 2, 13) This kind of serially antithetical statement (of which "The Thunder, Perfect Mind" is almost wholly composed) is in a style similar to that of the Round Dance, e.g., "I will be born and I will bear, amen. I will eat and I will be eaten, amen. I will hear and I will be heard, amen." etc. These sequential self-predications are very probably liturgical, spoken aloud by perfected persons who identify themselves as both divine and human. This would be entirely in accord with the gnostic Christian idea of Jesus as a mirror. For them Jesus was a form of self-discovery and not a particular male divine person. For a "bride of Christ" in this sense, it would make sense to assert that "I am she whose wedding is great, and I have not taken a husband. I am the solace of my labor

17. Quotations from the Nag Hammadi Codex are taken from J. Robinson ed., *The Nag Hammadi Library*.

pains [having given birth within herself to her bridegroom]. I am the bride and the bridegroom, and it is my husband who begot me." Another style of self-predication, reminiscent of the passage quoted above from the Acts of Xanthippe 14, can be found in the "Trimorphic Protennoia" (N.H.C. xiii, 1): "I am the Protennoia, the Thought that dwells in the light. I am the movement that dwells in the All, she in whom the All takes its stand, the first-born among those who came to be, she who exists before the All. . . . I am a Voice [speaking softly]. I exist [from the first, I dwell] within the Silence [that surrounds every one of them]. And [it is] the [hidden Voice] that [dwells within] me, [within the] intangible, immeasurable Thought, within the immeasurable Silence" (xiii, 1, 35–36). As it is not our purpose here to do a full study of liturgical gnostic self-predications we shall not attempt to discuss them as they appear in both the apocryphal Acts and the Nag Hammadi Codexes at any length. It will suffice to say that the gnostic influences apparent in some of the Acts derive from a religious tradition exalting both the female and the male aspects of divinity and that such influences appear most obviously in the more liturgical passages of the Acts.

In the early church there was, within both "orthodox" and "gnostic" circles, a strong undercurrent of thought that stressed androgyny as a primary symbol of spiritual completion. The classic inquiry into this symbolic realm is that of Wayne Meeks, "The Image of the Androgyne: Some Uses of a Symbol in Earliest Christianity." He writes that "Galatians 3:28 contains a reference to the 'male and female' of Genesis 1:27 and suggests that somehow the act of Christian initiation reverses the fateful division of Genesis 2:21–22. Where the image of God is restored, there, it seems, man is no longer divided—not even by the most fundamental division of all, male and female. The baptismal reunification formula thus belongs to the familiar *Urzeit–Endzeit* pattern, and it presupposes an interpretation of the creation story in which the divine image after which Adam was modeled was masculofeminine."[18] He finds this kind of thinking particularly present in what he terms the "Encratite" circles which produced apocryphal Acts.

18. Meeks, "The Image of the Androgyne," *History of Religions* 13 no. 3 (February 1974):185.

The virgin Thecla, for example, could be taken as the very model of a female who "makes herself male," and her donning of men's clothing, thus becoming what the Gospel of Thomas would call a *monachos*—not only a celibate, but also one who must break all ties to home, city, and ordinary society, becoming a wanderer. In the Encratite Acts, the ascetic life is idealized as that of an itinerant, whose baptism liberates him from "the world," understood primarily as sexuality and society.[19]

In Encratite circles, reunification was spiritualized and individualized to speak, apparently, of the transcendent self-consciousness of the gnostic. It became the sign not so much of a sect as of the radically isolated individual, who, by leaving behind the differentia of male and female, leaves behind the cosmos itself—empirically speaking, the world of settled society. In both cases the reunification of male and female became a symbol for "metaphysical rebellion," an act of "cosmic audacity" attacking the conventional picture of what was real and what was properly human.[20]

But, like all extreme ideals, this ideal faded with the passage of time. The "world of settled society" can never be left wholly behind. By the fourth century ascetic monks of both sexes were beginning to band together into institutionalized single-sex communities.

As the *fathers* of the church imposed males-only restrictions on church leadership and on God the gnostic style of Christianity began to be defined as heresy. Elaine Pagels, in her book *The Gnostic Gospels*, observes that "Every one of the secret texts which gnostic groups revered was omitted from the canonical collection, and branded as heretical by those who called themselves orthodox Christians. By the time the process of sorting the various writings ended—probably as late as the year 200—virtually all the feminine imagery for God had disappeared from the orthodox Christian tradition."[21] The early Christian church appears to have experienced conflicts between Christian men and Christian women which oc-

19. Ibid., p. 196.

20. Ibid., p. 207; see also the appendix to Richard Batey, *New Testament Nuptial Imagery*, and R. M. Grant, "The Mystery of Marriage in the Gospel of Philip," *Vigiliae Christianae* 15(1961):129–40.

21. Pagels, *The Gnostic Gospels*, p. 57.

curred along both sexual and conceptual lines. Eventually the male hierarchy won out. It is their Christianity we have today.

The Acts, if they are what remain of a burst of creativity among Christian women of very early times, are valuable for our time. They appear to have been a striving by Christian women for both a mode of self-expression and a way to preach rebellion for the sake of continence. Just as women of the present day seek to obtain equal standing with men in Christian churches, so did the Christian women of the second century. If our argument that the apocryphal Acts originated in communities of continent Christian women should achieve general acceptance, matristics will be a possibility.

Bibliography

Abbott, Frank F. *Society and Politics in Ancient Rome*. New York: Scribner's Sons, 1909.

Achtemeier, Paul J. "Jesus and the Disciples as Miracle Workers in the Apocryphal New Testament." In *Aspects of Religious Propaganda in Judaism and Early Christianity*, edited by Elisabeth Schüssler Fiorenza. Notre Dame, Ind.: Notre Dame University Press, 1976.

Bangerter, L. N. *Frauen im Aufbruch*. Neukirchen-Vluyn: Neukirchener Verlag, 1971.

Batey, Richard. *New Testament Nuptial Imagery*. Leiden: Brill, 1971.

Bauer, Walter. *Rechtglaubigkeit und Ketzerei im ältesten Christentum*. Tübingen: Mohr, 1934.

Brown, Peter. *Religion and Society in the Age of Saint Augustine*. London: Faber and Faber, 1972.

Chadwick, H. "Enkrateia." In *Reallexicon für Antike und Christentum*. Vol. 5. Stuttgart: Hiersemann, 1962.

Craigie, W. A., trans. "The Acts of Xanthippe and Polyxena." In *The Ante-Nicene Christian Library*, *Additional Volume*, edited by Allan Menzies. New York: Christian Literature Co., 1896.

Dodds, E. R. *Pagan and Christian in an Age of Anxiety*. Cambridge: At the University Press, 1965.

Douglas, Mary. *Natural Symbols*. London: Barrie and Jenkins, 1973.

———. *Purity and Danger*. London: Routledge & Kegan Paul, Ltd., 1966.

Encyclopedia of Religion and Ethics, s.v. "Encratites."

Fiorenza, Elisabeth Schüssler. "Word, Spirit and Power." In *Women of Spirit*, edited by Rosemary Ruether. New York: Simon and Schuster, 1979.

Friedländer, Ludwig. *Roman Life and Manners*. New York: Barnes and Noble, 1965.

Gager, John. *Kingdom and Community*. Englewood Cliffs, New Jersey: Prentice Hall and Co., 1975.

Goodenough, Erwin. *Jewish Symbols in the Greco-Roman Period*. Vol. 4. New York: Pantheon Books, 1953.

Grant, R. M. "The Mystery of Marriage in the Gospel of Philip." *Vigiliae Christianae* 15(1961):129–40.

Gryson, Roger. *The Ministry of Women in the Early Church*. Collegeville, Minnesota: Liturgical Press, 1976.

Haight, Elizabeth. *More Essays on Greek Romances*. New York: Longmans, Green and Co., 1945.

James, Montague R. "Acta Xanthippae et Polyxenae." In *Apocrypha Anecdota, Texts and Studies*. Vol. 2, no. 3. Cambridge: At the University Press, 1893.

———. *The Apocryphal New Testament*. Oxford: Clarendon Press, 1924.

Jensen, Adolph. *Myth and Cult among Primitive Peoples*. Chicago: University of Chicago Press, 1963.

Kelly, J. N. D. *Early Christian Creeds*. New York: McKay Co., 1960.

Klijn, A. F. J. *The Acts of Thomas*. Leiden: Brill, 1962.

Kropp, Angelicus M. *Ausgewählte Koptische Zaubertexte*. Vols. 1 and 2. Brussels: Edition de la Fondation reine Elizabeth, 1930.

Laeuchli, Samuel. *The Serpent and the Dove*. Nashville, Tenn.: Abingdon Press, 1966.

Lightfoot, J. B. *The Apostolic Fathers, Part One*. Vol. 1. London: Macmillan, 1890.

Lipsius, R. A. *Die Apokryphen Apostelgeschichte und Apostellegenden*. Vols. 1 and 2. Brunswick, Germany, 1883–1890.

McKenna, Mary Lawrence. *Women of the Church*. New York: Kenedy Co., 1967.

MacMullen, Ramsay. *Enemies of the Roman Order*. Cambridge: Harvard University Press, 1966.

Mair, Lucy. *Witchcraft*. New York: McGraw-Hill, 1969.

Marwick, Maxwell. *Sorcery in Its Social Setting*. Manchester: Manchester University Press, 1965.

Meeks, Wayne. "The Image of the Androgyne." *History of Religions* 13(1974):165–208.

Nugent, Rosamond M. *Portrait of the Consecrated Woman in Greek Christian Literature of the First Four Centuries*. Washington, D.C.: Catholic University of America Press, 1941.

Pagels, Elaine. *The Gnostic Gospels*. New York: Random House, 1979.

Parvey, Constance F. "The Theology and Leadership of Women in the New Testament." In *Religion and Sexism*, edited by Rosemary Ruether. New York: Simon and Schuster, 1974.

Perkins, Pheme. "Peter in Gnostic Revelation." In *Society of Biblical Literature 1974 Seminar Papers*, edited by George MacRae. Vol. 2. Missoula, Mont.: Scholar's Press, 1974.

Peterson, Peter M. *Andrew, Brother of Simon Peter: His History and His Legends*. Leiden: Brill, 1958.

Preaux, Claire. "Le statut de la femme à l'époque hellénistique, principalement en Égypte." In *La Femme, Recueil de la Société Jean Bodin* 11, no. 1 (1959).

Preisendanz, Karl. *Papyri Graecae Magicae*. Vols. 1 and 2. Leipzig: G. Teubner, 1928.

Pulver, Max. "Jesus' Round Dance and Crucifixion According to the Acts of John." Vol. 2 in *The Mysteries: Papers from the Eranos Yearbooks*, edited by Joseph Campbell. Bollingen Series. 30 vols. Princeton: Princeton University Press, 1955.

Quasten, Johannes. *Patrology*. Vol. 1. Utrecht: Spectrum, 1950.

Quispel, Gilles. "An Unknown Fragment of the Acts of Andrew." *Vigiliae Christianae* 10(1956):129–48.

———. *Makarius, das Thomasevangelium und das Lied von der Perle*. Leiden: Brill, 1967.

Reitzenstein, R. *Hellenistische Wundererzählungen*, Darmstadt: Wissenschaftliche Buchgesellschaft, 1963.

Report of the Archbishop of Canterbury's Committee on the Ministry of Women. *The Ministry of Women*. London: Society for Promoting Christian Knowledge, 1919.

Riddle, M. B., trans. "Two Epistles Concerning Virginity." In *The Ante-Nicene Christian Fathers*, edited by A. Roberts and J. Donaldson. Vol. 8. Grand Rapids, Mich.: Eerdmans, 1951.

Robinson, James M., ed. *The Nag Hammadi Library*. Leiden: Brill, 1977.

Rohde, Erwin. *Der Griechische Roman und seine Vorläufer*. Hildesheim: Olms Verlag, 1960.

Ruether, Rosemary. "Mothers of the Church: Ascetic Women in the Late Patristic Age." In *Women of Spirit*, edited by Rosemary Ruether. New York: Simon and Schuster, 1979.

―――. "Virginal Feminism in the Fathers of the Church." In *Religion and Sexism*, edited by Rosemary Ruether. New York: Simon and Schuster, 1974.

―――, ed. *Women of Spirit*. New York: Simon and Schuster, 1979.

Ryrie, Charles. *The Role of Women in the Church*. Moody Press, 1958.

Schmidt, Karl. *Kanonische und Apokryphe Evangelien und Apostelgeschichten*. Basel: Verlag von Heinrich Majer, 1944.

Schneemelcher, Wilhem, and Hennecke, Edgar, eds. *New Testament Apocrypha*. Vol. 2. English translation edited by R. McL. Wilson. Philadelphia: The Westminster Press, 1966.

Söder, Rosa. *Die apokryphen Apostelgeschichten und die romanhafte Literatur der Antique*. Stuttgart: W. Kohlhammer Verlag, 1932.

Souter, A. "The 'Acta Pauli' etc. in Tertullian." *Journal of Theological Studies* 25(1924):292.

Stählin, "Chēra." In *Theological Dictionary of the New Testament*, edited by G. Friedrich. Vol. 9. Grand Rapids, Mich.: Eerdmans, 1974.

Swidler, Leonard. "Greco-Roman Feminism and the Reception of the Gospel." In *Traditio-Krisis-Renovatio aus Theologischen Sicht*, edited by B. Jaspert and R. Mohr. Marburg: Elwert Verlag, 1976.

Theissen, Gerd. *Sociology of Early Palestinian Christianity*. Philadelphia: Fortress Press, 1978.

Tucker, Robert C. "The Theory of Charismatic Action." *Daedalus* 97(Summer 1968):731–54.

Von Campenhausen, H. *Die Askese im Urchristentum*. Tubingen, 1949.

Von Harnack, Adolph. *The Mission and Expansion of Christianity in the First Three Centuries*. New York: Putnam Press, 1908.

Vööbius, M. *A History of Asceticism in the Syrian Orient*. 2 vols. Louvain, 1960.

Vouaux, Léon. *Les Actes de Pierre*. Paris: Librairie Letouzey, 1922.

Weber, Max. *From Max Weber, Essays in Sociology*, edited and translated by H. H. Garth and C. W. Mills. New York: Oxford University Press, 1958.

Index

135